50 GREAT JAMAICAN SPORTS STARS

Rodney Hinds and Joel Campbell

This edition published in Great Britain in 2013 by DB Publishing, an imprint of JMD Media.

ISBN 9781780913179

Printed and bound by Copytech (UK) Limited, Peterborough.

50 GREAT JAMAICAN SPORTS STARS

Rodney Hinds and Joel Campbell

CONTENTS

RADHA = BHAUANI

Acknowledgements

There have been so many that have contributed to this book. They include
Jermaine Haughton, John Portch, Ernest Simons, Ken Passley, Colin Patterson,
Lennox Smillie, Chantelle Azille, Barbara Colossi, Rosalind Burke,
Doreen Hodges, among others.

Foreword by Donovan Bailey

Its an amazing honour to be in the company of anything that is great and one of the particular things is that the tiny island of Jamaica has produced some of the most incredible sports people in the history of this planet. So to be a part of that and to be a part of this book, 50 Great Jamaican Sports Stars, it's a great honour.

I think in the next 50 years it gets way bigger because we are going to dominate track and field full stop. Jamaica and Jamaican born (athletes) will dominate track and field for the next fifty years we know that.

But I think with baseball, basketball, football and even hockey there is massive room.

I live in Jamaica during the winter and I see a lot of kids who are swimmers, tennis players, basketball and baseball players and going forward we will be more dominant and I am looking forward to that!

Former 100m world record holder

Jamaica sport round up

Jamaica continues to punch above its weight across a multitude of sporting disciplines.

For more than six decades sportsmen and women from a nation of less than 3 million have stunned the world with their remarkable feats in athletics, cricket and boxing in addition to less heralded forays into football, basketball and even winter sports.

Since Arthur Wint and Herb McKenley ushered in a dominant era for Jamaican athletics with their respective gold and silver medals in the 400m at the 1948 Olympics, the country has won 17 Olympic gold medals, 67 in total, and currently possesses the fastest human being of all time in Usain Bolt.

Wint, who also celebrated silver in the 800m in London, returned alongside McKenley in Helsinki in 1952 as Jamaica won the 4x400m relay. Team-mate George Rhoden took gold in the 400m as Jamaica claimed eight medals in two Games.

Don Quarrie was next with his gold in the 100m at the 1976 Olympics, before a series of near misses, as wonderful athletes such as Grace Jackson, Juliet Cuthbert, Merlene Ottey and Winthrop Graham claimed a host of medals in the 1980s and 1990s.

Deon Hemmings took gold in the 400m hurdles at Atlanta in 1996 but this period seems fallow in comparison to what the late 2000s had in store as a host of home-trained Jamaican Olympians delivered a golden era that surpassed even the exploits of Wint, McKenley and Rhoden.

With 23 medals across the 2008 Beijing and 2012 London Olympics Jamaica thrust itself to the forefront of world athletics through the exploits of Usain Bolt, Yohan Blake, Shelly-Ann Fraser-Pryce, and Melanie Walker amongst others.

From the mid-1970s until the early 1990s the West Indies could lay claim to the finest side in Test and limited-overs cricket history. It is a lofty perch from which Jamaica has a leg to stand on given the contributions of Michael Holding, Jeff Dujon and Courtney Walsh.

Today the island can currently lay claim to the most devastating batsmen across all formats with former captain Chris Gayle, who was part of the West Indies side to lift the World T20 in 2012.

When it comes to Jamaican boxing the island's prowess extends beyond the heavyweight division. Jamaica's Mike McCallum won world titles in three different weight categories in the 1980s.

There has also been global success for Glen Johnson, who claimed the IBF light heavyweight title in 2004 before going on to famously knock-out Roy Jones Junior.

Any perusal of Jamaican boxing is incomplete without reference to the legendary Bunny Grant, who was the first Jamaican to fight for a world title in 1964, when he met Eddie Perkins in Kingston.

Jamaica's slave and west African heritage has contributed to the nation's sporting excellence and it is not difficult to chart the success of ex-patriots and those sports people of Jamaican lineage.

Kingston has contributed four-time Olympic gold medallist for the United States Sanya Richards-Ross, Patrick Ewing, one of the greatest basketball players in NBA history, and John Barnes, the midfielder who is still fondly remembered for his wonderful exploits for Liverpool and England. St Catherine born Donovan 'Razor' Ruddock is remembered for his clashes with Mike Tyson.

There is also a host of Jamaican descendents throughout the English football pyramid, while boxing world champion Lennox Lewis can also claim roots on the island.

Less renowned than the fabled 1988 bobsled team is Lascelles Brown, who won silver for Canada in the two-man event at the 2010 Winter Olympics.

To add a further sheen Olympic gold medallists of Jamaican parentage on at least one side include Linford Christie, Donovan Bailey, Denise Lewis and Jessica Ennis-Hill.

With the West Indies cricket team winning their first major competition in almost a decade there is hope that Jamaica can help restore the international side's lustre.

Jamaican sport is in a good place and likely to get better.

About the authors

RODNEY HINDS

For some sports is a competitive career, for others it's a likeable pastime but for Rodney Hinds, currently the Sports & Features Editor of The Voice Newspaper, sports brings cohesion, pride and hope to millions of people worldwide.

In 1999 Rodney was co-author of 'Black Pearls - an A-Z of Black Footballers in the English Game'. In recent times Rodney has penned his second book 'Black Lions – The Story of Black Footballers in England.'

His contribution to sports journalism was recognised when he won the Black Plus+ 'Best Print Journalist' and Victoria Mutual 'Services to Cricket' awards.

Having launched his television career on BBC Breakfast Time, Rodney has also contributed and appeared on various sporting documentaries 'Black Flash – A Century of Black footballers in Britain' (BBC3), 'Daley Thompson' (BBC2) and 'Mike Tyson' (C4). He has appeared on Sky Sports and Soccer Sunday (ITV), was the sports pundit for CBBC TV Xchange children's programme and frequently acts as sports analyst for BBC TV and radio including regular stints on Radio Five Live, Talksport, BBC 1Xtra, BBC London 94.9, FM Choice FM and Radio Leicester, BBC Birmingham and BBC Three Counties Radio in Luton.

Among his big name interviews are Viv Richards, Lennox Lewis, Kobe Bryant, Thierry Henry and Jessica Ennis to name a few.

In recent times Rodney has covered the London 2012 Olympic Games. He is a regular in Premier League press boxes and has covered World Cup football and cricket, Wimbledon, Commonwealth Games, World Championship athletics and boxing bouts.

As well as writing, Rodney is also a motivational and passionate public speaker. Rodney was the first role model for the East Enders Academy, an organisation which takes inspirational men in to schools in order to boost the aspiration of young people.

Away from sport he likes to travel, music, cinema and good conversation.

Rodney is determined to share his experiences with others, hence his regular public speaking role with positive energy at the heart of his talks.

JOEL CAMPBELL

Joel Campbell is an ardent lover of a multiple sports and an avid reader and writer.

50 Great Jamaican Sports Stars represents his first noteworthy foray into authorship.

It was the demise of his personal dream to compete at sports highest level that helped to spawn an utter determination for him to follow the highs and lows of professional athletes all over the world, using the media as a platform and his prose as the vehicle.

A fifteen-year long career in journalism, where Joel has touched every media facet from written press and radio broadcasting to television and advancements in online technology, has enabled the Londoner to build up a plethora of sporting and commercial contacts from around the world.

Joel has contributed to most British national newspapers, BBC News (TV), BBC Radio Five Live, BBC World Service, Sky Sports, Ghana TV (GTV), Peace FM (Ghana), Choice FM (Ghana) Choice FM (UK), Irie FM (Jamaica) The Voice Newspaper (UK), The Gleaner Newspaper (Jamaica) and many more across the globe. Joel is a staunch advocate of sport being a great leveller.

To date Joel is still the only Rastafarian sports writer in the UK and regularly reports on premier events. Passionate about inclusion, Joel, a winner of the 2008 Football Black List award, consistently champions the positives gleaned from embracing a multi-cultural press box.

A founding member of the Black Collective of Media In Sport (BCOMS), Joel regards his work promoting a career in the media amongst the UK's black and minority ethnic (BAME) communities, as 'a job for life'.

Upon completing 50 Great Jamaican Sports Stars Joel said: "The endeavours experienced by all of those in this book are humbling. The obvious achievements such as winning medals and breaking records are there for all to applaud but it is the subtle, unspoken elements of these sports men and women's journeys that can at times leave you awestruck.

"There truly are no limits, if you want it enough and are prepared to make the sacrifices necessary, you can do in life everything you desire. This reality is a recurring theme throughout 50 Great Jamaican Sports Stars. I salute every one of the sports men and women in this book, as I do every sportsman and woman that embarks on a similar journey. Respect always."

Men's 4x400m 1952

Quartet: Arthur Wint, Herb McKenley, George Rhoden, Leslie Laing

If ever a moment signified the emergence of Jamaica in international track and field, it was the 1952 4x400m relay Olympic final in Helsinki.

National heroes Arthur Wint and Herb McKenley, were teamed with the lesser known but equally notable, George Rhoden and Leslie Laing to form a formidable quartet which won the gold medal, running a world record time of 3:03:9 – the only team other than that of the USA to hold a world record in the event.

As well as providing the perfect note to a championship that included George Rhoden leading a Jamaican one-two with Herb McKenley in the individual 400m, Wint's silver in the 800m and McKenley winning his second silver in the closest 100m in Olympic history – the island of 2.7million people was firmly on the map.

After some encouraging performances in previous Olympic Games, with an increasing number of Jamaicans who were then either studying in American universities and colleges, the 1952 relay team were favoured to compete well against their track rivals, to this very day, USA.

In the 1948 Olympics, the first post-war, the 4x400m relay, in front of some 80,000 expectant onlookers, saw Rhoden fly out of the blocks managing to keep level with American, Arthur Harnden, however former member of the Royal Air Force 23 year old Laing started to slip behind the lead of Cliff Bourland in the second leg.

Charged with eating up the deficit, in the penultimate leg, Wint stormed with intent in catching Roy Cochran but before he could pass on the baton to the waiting McKenley, on the final leg, Wint succumbed to injury, slumping to the track. The dream was over- and the USA were gold medal victors once again.

With vengeance on their mind, the same four men lined up in 1952 determined to make amends and bring home the Olympic gold medal.

Wint took over the first leg this time, in 46.8 seconds, and narrowly behind the USA's Ollie Matson, before passing the baton to Laing, who lagged further behind the Americans, leaving 15 metres for McKenley to cut down.

Deterred by the previous mistake at an identical point in London 1948, he ran a very controlled but explosive 44.6 third leg – putting finisher Rhoden with a chance of winning the gold for Jamaica. Faced by 800m specialist Whitfield, he stormed across the finishing line – sparking jubilant celebrations of an historic Jamaican relay victory.

Did you know?
- Representing the athletes who formed Jamaica's relay gold-medal-winning team at the 1952 Olympics, an enormous sculpture of a runner leaving the blocks, called "The Jamaican Athlete", was built outside the National Stadium at Independence Park in Kingston.
- Eager to give back Herb McKenley turned his hand to coaching once his career had finished taking his knowledge to his alma mater, Calabar High School.

1988 Jamaica bobsleigh team

The team: Devon Harris, Chris Stokes, Dudley Stokes, Michael White

On occasion sporting reality is fanciful enough without being moulded into a Hollywood film.

The Jamaican bobsleigh team that competed at the 1988 winter Olympics in Calgary represented a classic tale of the underdog overcoming considerable obstacles and haphazard preparation to take centre stage.

By the time of their ill-fated third run in the four-man event 'Jamaica 1' were at the centre of a media furore, as the global public became enchanted by the notion of a tropical nation, resplendent in their black, gold and green, competing in the monochrome world of winter sport.

The Jamaica Bobsleigh Federation was founded in 1987 by Jamaica-based American businessmen George Fitch and William Maloney who, inspired by a local pushcart race, felt that Jamaican athletic prowess could help them fashion a bobsleigh team.

Fitch asked the Jamaican Defence Force for volunteers. This process saw the recruitment of Dudley Stokes, Devon Harris and Michael White. The trio were later joined by Caswell Allen.

Training on alpine tracks across the globe was difficult for a crew that had not set foot on ice six months prior to the Olympics.

Just days before their first race in Calgary, Allen turned his ankle on a frozen lake and was replaced by Dudley Stokes' brother, Chris.

The younger Stokes was only in Calgary to support his sibling, yet he was a noted sprinter and was quickly inducted into the crew.

An inconspicuous performance in the two-man event and the calamitous first races of the four-man competition did not dent the team's popularity within the Olympic fraternity.

Contrary to their depiction in the hit movie Cool Runnings, the Jamaicans gained support and advice from their fellow competitors.

The crew entered Olympic legend with their final run. The team posted the seventh-fastest push start of the competition but driver Dudley Stokes, who was carrying a shoulder injury, soon lost control of the sled.

Turn nine was a Kriesel, which is a turn that rotates a sled through at least 270 degrees. The sled came out of the Kriesel upside down at 85mph.

The athletes' heads collided with the surface and the sled threw up a stream of ice as it careened around the track carried by its momentum.

Yet the crew were relatively unhurt and with the polite applause of onlookers filling the air they strolled towards the finish line ahead of their sled.

A bigger reception greeted the new national heroes upon their return to Jamaica.

Did you know?
- Jamaica came in 30th in the two-man event
- George Fitch approached the Jamaican Defence Force through Colonel Ken Barnes, father of Liverpool and England football legend, John
- Each man competed at Albertville in France four years later, while the Stokes brothers and Harris continued until the 1998 Nagano Winter Olympics.

1998 Jamaica World Cup squad

The Reggae Boyz carved their name in Jamaican sporting history and captured public imagination with their battling performances at the 1998 World Cup.

Jamaica became the third Caribbean nation in history to qualify for the finals and with a population of 2.4 million were the smallest nation competing in France that summer.

Though the Reggae Boyz were outclassed by their Group H opponents Croatia and Argentina they bounced back to claim the maiden World Cup victory their efforts deserved with a 2-1 defeat of Japan in their final match.

Like Jamaica, and indeed Japan, Croatia were making their World Cup debut in their encounter in Lens, but whereas the bulk of the Jamaican squad was drawn from the nation's modest domestic league Croatia could call upon players from sides such as Real Madrid, AC Milan and Valencia.

Jamaica withstood the Balkan fluidity and menace until Igor Stimac rattled the crossbar from eight yards on 27 minutes. The rebound fell to Mario Stanic for whom the ball bobbled at first before the Parma midfielder was able to slot it home from point blank range.

The riposte came just before half-time when Robbie Earle headed Ricardo Gardner's cross beyond Drazen Ladic to bag an equaliser and send Jamaican fans across the world into raptures.

Alas, Davor Suker and Robert Prosinecki demonstrated Croatia's greater experience and superiority with second half goals in an eventual 3-1 victory.

The gulf in quality was even more profound when the Reggae Boyz met Argentina in Paris in their second match.

Ariel Ortega's brace and Gabriel Batistuta's 11-minute hat-trick inflicted a 5-0 mauling, yet the floodgates only opened with the sending off of Darryl Powell for a second yellow card in first-half stoppage-time.

Both Jamaica and Japan were out but their meeting in Lyon gave each a chance to depart with a victory.

Theodore Whitmore opened the scoring in the 39th minute when captain Ian Goodison's long ball was knocked on by Marcus Gayle and fell to the Seba United midfielder, who lashed a drive into the bottom corner from inside the Japanese penalty area.

Whitmore doubled his tally on 54 minutes when he drove down the right flank, cut inside Norio Imura, and drilled a fierce six-yard drive past goalkeeper Nobuyuki Kojima.

Japan reduced the arrears with Masashi Nakayama's 74th minute effort but the Reggae Boyz were not to be denied.

Reaching the World Cup had been their finest achievement and Jamaica left clutching a cherished victory.

Did you know?

- Jamaica's 1-0 World Cup qualifying defeat of Mexico in Kingston in November 1996 was their first victory over the Central American giants and ensured their progress to the final CONCACAF qualifying round for first time;

- Eight of Jamaica's 22-man squad were born overseas: Marcus Gayle, Fitzroy Simpson, Robbie Earle, Deon Burton, Frank Sinclair, Darryl Powell and Paul Hall were born in England and Andy Williams was born in Toronto, Canada.

Men's 4x100m relay team 2012

Quartet: Usain Bolt, Yohan Blake, Nesta Carter and Michael Frater

Fifty years after the independence, and six decades following the nation's first Olympic relay gold medal, the Jamaican 4x100m relay team gave their compatriots further reason to celebrate.

Ripping apart the previous world record time of 37.04, they set in the World Championships, a year earlier, the 2012 Olympic quartet raised the bar again with a new marker of 36.84.

The extraordinary feat is underlined by the fact the American team (starring Trell Kimmons, Justin Gatlin, Tyson Gay and Ryan Bailey) equalled the previous world record, thus recording the second fastest time ever – yet still finished as the bridesmaids.

As 'The Beast' Blake passed the baton to the irrepressible 'Lighting' Bolt, one of the American bright young hopes, the rangy Bailey was narrowly ahead – by just a metre.

However, the Trelawny native, showed the class that led to successful 100m and 200m defences in London, shredding Bailey down the home stretch to yet another Jamaican sprint victory.

Veteran Asafa Powell was unable to run in the race because of a groin injury, but the younger Jamaicans were able to pick up the slack.

Powell wasn't a part of the relay team's world-record effort back in 2011, but most expected him to handle one of the legs in London.

He was the anchor in Beijing and ended up finishing off Jamaica's golden performance four years ago.

As the baton-debacle in Athens 2004 showed, having the fastest team members isn't all that counts in the relay competition, however with the experience of Jamaica team captain Michael Frater and consistency of Nesta Carter – both in their first races at London 2012 – combined with the raw exuberance of Blake and strut of Bolt, their co-operation brought the best from each competitor.

The Jamaican sprint team had once again taken the breath and the eyes of the 80,000 seated in the London Olympic Stadium and the billions watching worldwide, again pushing the boundaries of their sport on the biggest stage possible.

Did you know?

- Usain Bolt celebrated with a "Mobot" as he crossed the line, paying tribute to Britain's 5,000m and 10,000m double Olympic champion, Mo Farah
- Following the withdrawal of Powell through injury, the last available reserve for the Jamaican team was Kemar Bailey-Cole, a 20 year-old up-and-coming athlete
- The Jamaican 4x100m relay team have now won five consecutive Olympic and World Championships since 2008

Gerry Alexander

Born: November 2, 1928 – April 16, 2011
Place of birth: Kingston

There was a time when Gerry Alexander seemed an unlikely Jamaican hero.

The Kingston-born wicketkeeper remains the last white man to captain the West Indies and assumed the role in 1957 when Jamaica was still ruled from Westminster and black emancipation had yet to be fully realised.

His appointment was perceived to be another case of white over promotion in the face of the supposedly more credible candidacies of Clyde Walcott and Everton Weekes.

It did not help that Alexander's early forays in Test cricket were ignominious. Tension increased when Alexander sent home Roy Gilchrist for ill discipline on the West Indies 1958-9 tour of India after Gilchrist had been warned about his overly aggressive bowling.

A same sense of decency that enabled him to hand over the captaincy to Frank Worrell in 1960 and serve as the Barbadian's right-hand man when Worrell returned from university.

Ultimately, the distinction with which Alexander kept wicket was allied to a solid batting technique that saw the right-hander labelled a pioneer wicketkeeper-batsman.

His 25 Test caps took in the 1960-61 West Indies tour of Australia where as deputy to Worrell he scored 484 runs (then a record for a wicketkeeper), recorded his only first-class century with a 108 in Sydney, and participated in the first-ever 'Tied Test' in Brisbane.

Australia needed six runs and had three wickets in hand with Wes Hall coming in to bowl the final eight-ball over – then a tradition in Australia – of the final day's play.

Alexander pounced on Richie Benaud's feeble hook shot on the second ball and stumped Wally Grout on the sixth.

Australia needed one run off the two remaining balls but Joe Solomon ran out Ian Meckiff on the next to ensure the tie.

That series, which saw Australia run out 2-1 victors is regarded as one of the finest in Test history.

Its edifying mix of outstanding attacking play, unprecedented drama, and sportsmanship has been said to have 'saved' cricket at a time when the sport found itself in the doldrums.

Upon learning of Alexander's death, aged 82, in April 2011, Benaud described him as "one of the finest wicketkeeper-batsmen I have ever seen."

Alexander's West Indies team-mate Solomon added: "He was a great friend of mine. He was a very likable person, the kind of man who you'd like to meet and be in his company."

Did you know?

- His full name was Franz Copeland Murray Alexander
- Alexander retired from cricket to become a vet and rose to the post of Chief Veterinary Officer of the Jamaican government
- He was also a talented footballer and won the FA Amateur Cup in 1953

Alia Atkinson

Born: December 11, 1988

Place of Birth: St Andrew

It's not just the medals and honours that define greatness in sport. Breaking new ground consistently throughout your career and inspiring a nation are also hallmarks of excellence, traits possessed by swimmer Alia Atkinson.

Jamaica is not renowned for producing swimmers despite the nation's healthy relationship with recreational aquatic activities due to the island being surrounded by both the Atlantic and Caribbean seas.

Nevertheless, Atkinson's eye-catching accomplishment at the London Olympic Games, where she finished fourth in the 100m women's breaststroke final, has literally inspired a nation.

Despite the fact she was only 23 years-old at the London 2012 Games it wasn't Atkinson's first foray on the Olympic stage, it was in fact her third. She had already qualified for and competed at the Athens 2004 and Beijing 2008 extravaganzas; Atkinson is an experienced competitor.

The youngest of all the swimmers at the 2004 Games, Atkinson ventured onto the biggest sporting platform in the world having created history by winning ten gold and one silver medal at the Caribbean Islands Swimming Championships (CISC) at the Jamaica National Stadium pool.

For many, missing out on a podium placing at an Olympic Games by one position might have derailed the rest of their season but testament to Atkinson's incessantly driven nature, the US-based athlete finished 2012 on a high by becoming the first ever Jamaican to win a medal at a global tournament when she finished second in the women's 50m breaststroke at the FINA World Short Course Swimming Championships. Her good form was compounded by a second silver medal, won in the women's 100 metres breaststroke.

Already the darling of her nation, Atkinson remains aware of the fact that apart from cyclist David Weller's amazing 1000-metre time trial bronze at the Moscow Olympics of 1980, no Jamaican has ever won an Olympic medal outside of athletics, this is a situation she aims to change.

Eyes firmly on bettering her Olympic performance in Brazil, 2016, Atkinson's presence in the pool looks to be one that the world will have to get used to.

Did You Know?
- Atkinson's mantra is: 'Hoping to improve youth swimming anywhere I can'
- She was only the 12th Jamaican swimmer to compete at an Olympic Games since 1968 and the first Jamaican swimmer of either gender to qualify for a breaststroke event at the 2004 Athens Olympics
- The Olympian graduated from Texas A&M University in 2010 with a Bachelor of Science degree in Psychology and minor in English

Donovan Bailey

Born: December 16, 1967

Place of Birth: Manchester, Jamaica

Financier, entrepreneur and Olympic champion, not a bad CV for Jamaica-born 100m sprinter Donovan Bailey – the fastest man in the world during the 90's.

Six years after fellow Canadian sprinter Ben Johnson disgraced the world of athletics in Seoul, Bailey restored honour and credibility to both his adopted nation and the sport winning the Olympic 100m final in 1996.

Breaking the world record in the process with a blistering time of 9.84 seconds in Atlanta, he doubled his efforts anchoring the Canadian 4x100m relay win over the Americans – whereby Bailey beat Dennis Mitchell to the tape by four metres.

Despite being the underdogs in the much anticipated 4x100m final, the Canadians who also included Bruny Surin, Robert Esmie and Glenroy Gilbert did not disappoint their fans, opening up a lead in the second leg, before the nation's most decorated sprinter, rode home to a historic victory.

Immigrating to Canada from Jamaica aged 13, Bailey initially was an eminent basketball player before graduation, only beginning to take track and field seriously in 1994. In fact, in his early adult years, his future seemed set to lie in the highly lucrative financial world, where he was charging up the corporate ladder as a successful stockbroker.

It was in the following year, in the Gothenburg-hosted World Championships that Bailey announced himself to the world, winning the 100m, breezing past compatriot Surin by 6/100th of a second, as well as aiding Canada's 4x100m relay team to victory.

Dubbed the 'sprinter of the decade', Bailey challenged 400m and 200m Olympic superstar Michael Johnson, who had also looked imperious

33

during the Atlanta Games, to a winner-takes-all race to see who was the world's fastest human.

Much hyped with trash talk between both athletes, Bailey won the race in 1997, over 150m, as Johnson pulled up with an injury halfway through, winning a reported $1.5million.

To cap an impressive year, financially and athletically, Bailey underlined his sprinting prowess taking a third world title with the Canadian relay team, and finishing second in the individual behind American Maurice Greene, opening up an intense rivalry between the two.

However, after being beset by niggling injures and ailments, Bailey was forced into retirement as Canada's greatest ever sprinter in 2001 – with five world and Olympic championship medals in his pocket.

Did you know?

- Bailey still holds the indoor world record in the 50 metres (5.56, in Reno, Nevada, in 1996),
- The sprinter retired in 2001 and now runs DBX Sport Management, a company that promotes amateur athletes. He has also started a sport injury clinic in Oakville, Ontario
- He has been inducted into Canada's Sports Hall of Fame twice: in 2004 as an individual, and in 2008 as part of the 1996 Summer Olympics 4x100 relay team

John Barnes

Born: November 7, 1963

Place of Birth: Kingston

John Barnes is the finest footballer that Jamaica has ever produced. The shame for many from the Caribbean is that he did not don the famous black, yellow and gold strip of his native Jamaica; rather he represented his 'adopted' England and gained 79 caps.

Fascinatingly his international career spawned much criticism and debate but no one could dispute his finest moment while wearing the badge of the Three Lions on his shirt. A quite sensational solo goal against the ultimate opponents, Brazil, in the famous Maracana Stadium in June 1984 will live in the memory for decades.

Barnes was quick, had a good football brain that was usually to the benefit of team-mates, and also had an eye for goal from open play or dead ball situations. He was exciting!

Barnes' football career began after gaining his education in Jamaica. On arrival to the UK he was soon scouted by Watford where team mate Luther Blissett would become his mentor. He signed for the club on July 14 1981. The rest is history.

The winger would go on to carve out an illustrious trophy-laden career with one of the biggest and most famous clubs in the world, Liverpool after signing for £900,000. In 292 appearances he won two First Division League Championships, two FA Cups and one League Cup.

Barnes' form was such that despite being surrounded by world-class players he was generally regarded as the star that shone brightest at Anfield. Personal accolades included twice winning the coveted Football Writers Association Footballer of the Year gong.

After leaving Liverpool he would end his glorious career with stints at Newcastle United and Charlton Athletic.

His managerial career was less successful. In 1999 he took charge of Scottish giants Celtic but injuries to key players and a shock defeat to minnows Inverness Caledonian Thistle ended in his sacking.

Barnes became the manager of his native Jamaica in September 2008, leading them to the Caribbean Championship months later.

In 2009, a decade after his Celtic days, he took over at Tranmere in before leaving the club after a run of poor results.

Barnes'status as a football icon was underlined in May 2013 when as part of the Royal Mail's celebration of 150 years of the Football Association, he was among one of the 11 footballers recognised as the United Kingdom's greatest football heroes.

Did You Know?

- Barnes serves as an ambassador for the Save The Children organisation
- Ironically Barnes made his England debut when he came on as a second half replacement for compatriot and Watford team-mate Luther Blissett on May 28, 1983

Trevor Berbick

Born: August 1, 1954 – October 28, 2006

Place of birth: Norwich, Port Antonio

The sporting label of heavyweight champion of the world is the one that the sport's big men crave. For a time Trevor Berbick could bask in such glory.

In March 1986 Berbick captured the most coveted crown in sport when he beat Pinklon Thomas on a points decision at the Riviera Hotel & Casino, Las Vegas, Nevada. His reign was short as he was to be destroyed by an up-and-coming 'Iron' Mike Tyson in two savage rounds just eight months later.

While in the ring, Berbick – a strong puncher who moved well for a big man - had much to suggest that he would have had a long reign as world heavyweight boxing champion - except for the bad luck in the timing of his career.

Berbick moved to Canada (later taking Canadian citizenship) after representing his home island in the Olympic Games at Montreal in 1976.

He made his professional début in September 1976 and continued to box until a blood clot on the brain forced him to retire in June 2000. By then he had established a record of 62 contests - winning 50 (33 by knockout), 11 defeats and one draw.

Berbick was a tenacious pugilist. His first challenge for the World Boxing Council's (WBC) world heavyweight crown was unsuccessful when he was outpointed by Larry Holmes in 1981.

In the same year Berbick recorded a hollow victory against the biggest name in sport. In December he achieved his most famous victory by outpointing the three times world champion Muhammad Ali over 10 rounds at Nassau in the Bahamas. While it was a tell-your-grandchildren moment there was a genuine reason why he was able to beat the self-styled 'Greatest.'

Ali was a shadow of his former self but it was an illustrious notch on Berbick's belt as he won by a clear points margin. It was the last time that Ali was to fight.

During a noteworthy career, Berbick – who had a heart as big as a lion – will be remembered for his defeat of Ali and being vanquished in spectacular fashion by Tyson.

After leaving the sport, Berbick was murdered on October 28, 2006.

Did you know?
- C. Lloyd Allen, former President of the Jamaica Boxing Board, paid tribute to the boxer when he said: "Berbick was a fine athlete and human being. One, who in his way, made a difference"
- Berbick was the last man to fight Muhammad Ali
- The former champion has three sons: Quinn, Jamaal and Shawn

Yohan Blake

Born: December 26, 1989

Place of Birth: St James, Jamaica

A Beast of a sprinting specimen, Yohan Blake has certainly showed some athletic beauty, clawing his way to the higher echelons of world sprinting earning plaudits from fans and critics alike that he is 'the next Bolt'.

He is the rising star keeping the previously unflappable Usain Bolt on his toes, both in training and on the track having already shown, in what are still the rookie years of his career, his passion to be the fastest man that ever lived.

Jumping from the shadow of his illustrious training partner, the whipper-snapper announced himself to the world by becoming the world champion over 100m in 2011, in Daegu.

Displaying incredible mental strength and stability when his compatriot Bolt was infamously disqualified, he beat a world class field to become, at a mere 21 years and 245 days old, the youngest 100m world champion of all time, surpassing triple Olympic gold medalist, Carl Lewis.

Exhibiting his adaptability, the 'Beast' played his part in Jamaica's world record breaking 37.04 seconds sprint in the 4x100m relay final in South Korea, shattering their previous feat three years previous.

His exploits put his name firmly on the tongues of sport fans worldwide heading into the 2012 Olympic Games in London; further enforced by beating the previously unbeatable Bolt at 100m and 200m in the Jamaican national trials.

Faced with the fastest collection of sprinters to ever compete, Blake won silver in both the 100m and 200m, in addition to a gold medal - and another world record breaking time - in the 4x100m relay, in his very first Olympics.

Prior to all of this, Blake had already proved he was on his way to greatness when he posted the second fastest time in 200m history, in Brussels,

with a eye-watering personal best of 19.26; an improvement of more than half a second from his heights set in Monaco 2010.

Some would say that it was inevitable Blake would one day have the world at his feet, after all he was awarded the Austin Sealy Trophy for the most outstanding athlete, after setting the fastest time by a Jamaican junior sprinter over 100m (10.11 seconds) at the 2007 CARIFTA Games.

Having already proved to be world class in his discipline, the only question is, just how great will he be?

Did you know?

- Blake was a keen cricketer at school, with fast bowling his speciality.
- On 16 August 2012, Blake rang the bell at Lord's Cricket Ground, London to signify the start of the Third Investec Test Match between England and South Africa. He was the first non-professional cricketer to do this.
- In a break from tradition and the IOC rules, Blake wore a customised Richard Mille Tourbillion watch in the semi-finals and finals of the 100m at the London Olympic Games. The timepiece was worth $500,000.

Luther Blissett

Born: February 1, 1958

Place of Birth: Falmouth

Luther Blissett has guaranteed his place in Jamaica's football history. It was the affable Blissett who in 1982 became the first black footballer to score an international hat-trick for the senior England side.

Blissett, like a number of Jamaica-born players, had 'adopted' England after his family had settled in the United Kingdom.

He proved that he obviously has a sense of occasion as he chose his full international debut – a 9–0 win over Luxembourg, to register himself in Jamaica's sporting folklore.

Blissett had made his name at club level with Watford which was not too far from the family Home in Harlesden, north west London. The striker, whose stand out traits were strength, pace and tenacity, helped the club rise from English football's fourth tier to the First Division during a golden era in the 1980s. Blissett holds the club's all-time records for appearances and goals, having played 503 games and scoring 186 goals.

In June 1983 Blissett moved to Italian giants AC Milan for £1 million on the back of his goal-getting at Watford. It was a shock and lucrative move for Blissett. However, the transfer was not to work out. He was to return to Watford at just half the price for which he departed.

Blissett's other employers also included Bournemouth, Bury and Mansfield where he was to hang up his boots in 1994.

The Watford legend was to coach at the club from 1996 for a while but was moved on five years later. Blissett was keen to manage a bigger club but was frustrated in his many attempts.

His love for Watford remains unabated. Just prior to the club just failing to regain a place at football's top table – they lost to Crystal Palace in the Championship play-off final at Wembley in May 2013 – Blissett enthused: "I'm hoping that they can replicate the team that I played in.

"This time I'm hoping that with the owners that we have, and them wanting to be involved for the long haul, that if we can get to the Premier League we can stay there without putting the club in jeopardy."

Dissuliosioned with a lack of opportunity within the so-called beautiful game, Blissett turned his hand to motorsport setting up Team 48 Motorsport a sports car racing team which initially included ex Watford team mate John Barnes and former QPR, Newcastle and Spurs star Les Ferdinand.

Did you know?

- Blissett's media career has seen him provide expert analysis for both Eurosport and BBC Five Live
- The striker had three different spells with his beloved Watford between 1975-1993
- A popular football magazine programme on Sky Sports TV, refers to the area where fans of the week sit as the Luther Blissett Stand

Usain Bolt

Born: August 21, 1986

Place of birth: Trelawny, Jamaica

Whole books could be written merely filled with the superlatives describing the bright personality, the jovial swagger and, of course, blistering sprint performances from the man known as the 'Lightning Bolt'.

Described by US double Olympic champion Michael Johnson as "possibly the best ever," the 6' 5" muscle-bound machine has systematically ripped up virtually every conceivable feat in the 100m, 200m and 4x100m relay - redefining the scope on what is and isn't possible.

A microscopic number of people have the success, reverence, and influence, both nationally and internationally to be thought of in similar passage to the likes of Bob Marley and Marcus Garvey, however, having raked in an estimated $20million, retained his Olympic 100m and 200m titles in London, added the Moscow world titles to that mix and driven every young child to aspire to run fast, he has become one of Jamaica's most prized exports.

Under the guidance of coach Glen Mills, the 'Lightning Bolt' left the Beijing crowd breathless at the 2008 Olympic Games, destroying the world record, he had set earlier in the year in New York City, crossing the finishing line at 9.69 seconds – despite visibly slowing down 30-40ms from the finish.

He then emulated US great Carl Lewis also reigning triumphant in the 200m, demolishing Michael Johnson's 12-year world record with a scorching 19.30 seconds – in the face of a 0.9m/s headwind.

Notwithstanding doubts over his fitness, a 100m final false-start disqualification at the World Championships 2011 in Daegu and defeats in both his main events by his training-mate Yohan Blake at the Olympic trials, Bolt served his critics humble-pie, retaining his 100m and 200m Olympic titles with utter ease with times of 9.63 seconds and 19.32 seconds respectively.

Despite his obvious talents from a young age, Bolt's High School coach Pablo McNeil began the diamond-polishing, recalling incidents where he would leave the school grounds and retrieve him in Falmouth, a chief town of Trelawny, where he had taken a taxi to go flirt with girls.

In spite of this, in front of a rapturous home crowd in Kingston, aged just 15 years old, Bolt became the youngest ever world junior champion in 2002, running a victorious 20.61 seconds in his favoured event, the 200m.

Even with the plaudits and accolades he has attained Bolt still yearns for Muhammad Ali- type greatness.

Agent Ricky Simms said: "The good thing with Usain, is that he is never done, he wants to win more. Is he a legend already?

"I think he is, but we want him to continue to build on his legend status. If he stopped today he would be one of the greatest sportsmen that ever lived. But there is more to come."

Did you know?

- Bolt is a fan of Manchester United Football Club and his favourite United player of all time is Dutch striker Ruud van Nistelrooy
- Bolt operates his own restaurant in Jamaica called 'Tracks And Records'
- The sprinter is the first man to hold both the 100m and 200m world records since fully automatic time measurements became mandatory in 1977

Walter Boyd

Born: January 1, 1972

Place of birth: Allman Town, Kingston

Walter Boyd is and will probably be the most enigmatic footballer to ever come from the Jamaican shores.

Complexity personified, quite how it is that Boyd had such an impact on the global game is still a relative mystery.

Sport often cries out for the main protagonists to show a bit of character, this however, is not an observation that could ever be leveled at Boyd, who's character was vivacious yet often difficult to understand.

What was never in doubt as far as most Jamaicans were concerned was Boyd's talent.

The striker had flamboyance, a great eye for goal and could use either foot, attributes highly respected in his homeland.

Controversially selected for the famous Reggae Boyz squad, which competed in the France 1998 World Cup, Boyd didn't really make the impact in the tournament his legion of fans had hoped he would.

This was due, in part, to being brought on as a second-half substitute in all three group games as well as the fact the then coach Rene Simoes didn't really 'fancy' the forward.

Simoes was effectively forced to pick 'Blacka Pearl' Boyd, as he was affectionately referred to by his fans.

When the Brazil-born coach intimated that there might not be a place for Boyd in the squad that travelled to France, community unrest and road blockades were a regular sight in Jamaica as Boyd supporters vented their fury.

The hype was good for Boyd. Despite an indifferent World Cup he went on to secure moves to the US with Colorado Foxes (USA League) and Swansea City in England's Football League as a result of his involvement with the Reggae Boyz.

There have been few footballers who have courted so many headlines in the national game like the enigmatic Boyd and some say the current Jamaican Football Federation footballing infrastructure will struggle to produce such ever again.

Whether or not we see another Boyd or not, it is important to remember that true greatness is defined by the people and to the people of Jamaica, Walter Boyd warranted that moniker.

Did you know?

- Boyd's season at Swansea saw the Welsh club secure promotion from Division Three with the Jamaican striker weighing in with seven goals that season.
- His last international match was a July 2001 friendly against Saint Kitts and Nevis
- Boyd was capped 60 times for Jamaica

Steve Bucknor

Date of birth: May 31, 1946

Place of birth: Montego Bay

Top class sport cannot take place without top class officials. Cricket umpire Steve Bucknor was exactly that.

While the modest Bucknor might not want to be labelled 'a star' his instantly recognisable hat and on-field traits marked him out whatever was taking place during a day's play.

Legend has it that Bucknor only took to umpiring following repeatedly incorrect decisions against him and his teams while playing cricket in Jamaica.

Bucknor made his umpire debut in his native Kingston when he officiated in the West Indies – India Test at Sabina Park on April 28, 1989. He was to stand in his final Test some 128 matches later when South Africa played Australia at Cape Town, in March 2009.

Add Bucknor's 181 one-day internationals and it would be fair to say that he has overseen an awful lot of cricket and cricketers.

As pressure on teams and players to perform has grown, along with the financial rewards, Bucknor was a necessary constant within the game. He was deemed firm but fair by most of the players that came under his jurisdiction.

The giant Bucknor had, as so many officials developed over the years, a unique way of giving batsmen out; once decided he would give his trademark nod and apologetic smile before raising the dreaded finger and sending batsmen on their way.

The accolades have been many for 6' 3" Bucknor. He broke Dickie Bird's record of 66 Tests in 2002, before in March 2005 becoming the first umpire to stand in 100 Tests. Bucknor also stood in five successive World Cup finals from 1992 to 2007.

Bucknor once gave some of the errant West Indies players some advice, saying: "When you do well, you get paid. When you don't do well, you don't. So, you must now perform to be recognised properly, and that is not happening."

Cricket is a global game and the travelling and upheaval for players and officials like Bucknor does not sometimes get recognised as they do their jobs.

Bucknor gave an insight into an umpire's life when he revealed: "The travelling has been wearing me down. It's always been hard – getting from place to place has never been that easy. I won't miss that."

Cricket has certainly missed Steve Bucknor.

Did you know?
- The official was 42 when he stood in first Test match
- Bucknor also refereed in a football World Cup qualifier when El Salvador played Netherlands Antilles in 1998
- Elite umpire Asad Rauf once said that Bucknor was instrumental in developing his own career

Bert Cameron

Born: November 16, 1959

Place of Birth: Spanish Town, St Catherine

Proud carrier of the famous black, green and gold flag at the 1984 Olympic Games opening ceremony in the 'city of angels' Los Angeles, the effervescent quarter miler was a consistent presence, internationally, during a career that spanned more than 15 years.

A three-time Olympian, the 400m sprinter was a highly consistent figure in the late 70s and early 80s.

Cameron won the 400m title at the first World Championships in athletics, hosted in Helsinki in 1983.

Like many Jamaican track & field stars, he was schooled in the United States, where he was seemingly unbeatable, specifically marked by his crowning as NCAA national 400m champion both in and outdoors between 1980-1; making Cameron the 'one to watch'.

During this illustrious spell, he followed up his bronze medals in both the individual and the relay at the 1981 IAAF World Cup, with a blistering gold medal victory at the Commonwealth Games just a year later, becoming 400m champion.

Therefore, it was a shoe-in that he was named Jamaican Sportsperson of the year not once, but three times between 1981-83.

A model professional, Cameron relentlessly collected the top honours at regional level; winning gold at the Central American and Caribbean Championships of 1981 and 1982 before returning again in 1985 to collect a second place finish.

It was during this period he was immersed in a dogged sporting rivalry with Cuban Roberto Hernandez, who he steamed past in the 1987 Pan-American Games to record a silver medal, behind Raymond Pierre.

Post-retirement, Cameron has become a coach of the 400m discipline in Jamaica's capital, notably while working at Glen Mills' Racers Track Club.

He took on and looked after the likes of Jermaine Gonzales, who went on to break the national record in 2010.

Cameron was bestowed with the honour of being the senior coach of the Jamaican team during the World Championships in Daegu, South Korea in 2011, reflecting his rise to the top of the coaching scene, in addition to his previous glories.

In a 2004 interview with The Gleaner, Cameron gave credit to his college, the University of Texas at El Paso, for moulding him from a raw talent into an accomplished world-beating athlete, by saying that "Being in a professional setting made a lot of difference."

Did you know?
- Cameron's personal best in the 400m was 44.50 set in 1988
- Cameron was a member of the Jamaican 4x400m quartet that won silver medal at the 1988 Olympics in Seoul, South Korea

Veronica Campbell-Brown

Born: May 15, 1982

Place of Birth: Clarks Town, Trelawny, Jamaica

Regarded by many as the greatest female Jamaican sprinter of all time, the affectionately known, V.C.B is a seven-time Olympic medallist, competing in the 100m and 200m.

The sprinter has the honour of having won a medal at every Commonwealth, World Championship (indoor and outdoor) and Olympic Games tournament she has entered.

One of only eight athletes to win world championships at youth, junior, and senior level, the extremely driven racer conspicuously underlines Jamaica's claim to being the 'Sprint Factory', pushing the boundaries of the sport for well over a decade.

Born to nine siblings, V.C.B, attended Troy Primary and Vere Technical High School in Clarendon, before moving to the United States to study at the University of Arkansas.

Her first Olympic medal was won at Sydney 2000; a silver in the Jamaican 4x100m relay at just 18 years-old, alongside female sprint legend, Marlene Ottey, confirming her ability to reach the limits of her talents in a pressure-cooker track and field environment.

She became only the second woman in history to win two consecutive Olympic 200m events when she hustled-and-harried her way to victory at both the 2004 and 2008 Games, in Athens and Beijing respectively.

Ever since her immersion into the sprint ranks as a junior her performances have predominantly been pretty close to perfection.

In 1999, she won two gold medals, in the 100m and 4x100m relay at the inaugural IAAF World Youth Championships and became the first female

to win the sprint double at the IAAF World Junior Championships a year later.

A born winner, even at the veteran stage of her career she captured another Olympic individual medal in the 200m, a bronze, and celebrated a silver medal in the 4x100m relay at London 2012.

Unfortunately for VCB its unlikely that she will be universally saluted as a great due to her failed doping test in May, 2013. But on the island of Jamaica she will always be seen as a queen of the track.

Did you know?
- Off the track, she married fellow Jamaican sprint athlete, Omar Brown and they reside in Florida
- She was appointed as a UNESCO Goodwill Ambassador in late 2009, and stated that she would use the role to promote gender equity in sport
- Campbell-Brown's personal best of 21.74 seconds in the 200m ranks her in the all-time top ten in the world, and the third best among Jamaican women.

Linford Christie

Born: April 2, 1960

Place of Birth: St. Andrew

Physically imposing and armed with an unyielding mental fortitude, Linford Christie is one of Jamaica's greatest exported talents.

Few will forget Christie storming to his Olympic gold medal in the 100m at the 1992 Games in Barcelona aged 32.

Having made the podium in 1988 at the now infamous Ben Johnson-dominated Seoul Olympics, victory four years later was all the sweeter given the fact that it would be the last time he would race in an Olympic final.

Christie wasn't to know that it would be his last ever shot at landing an Olympic medal in the 100m, indeed he made the start line of the final in Atlanta 1996, only to false start twice which led to him being disqualified from the race.

Looking back at Christie's humble beginnings, which saw him follow his parents to the United Kingdom aged seven, it was impossible to know that he would set so many high standards along his career.

Without doubt being the oldest man ever to win the 100m Olympic title ranks up there with his most significant achievements.

However, it was a light-bulb moment aged 24, which propelled Christie onto the greatness that had always eluded him.

Stern words from coach Ron Roddan, who believed that Christie wasn't living up to his potential, proved to be the perfect antidote for the sprinter to go on and become European champion in 1986.

A measure of how much Christie improved was to be seen in his personal best over 100m, which dropped from 10.42s in 1985 to 10.04s in 1986.

As far as Europe goes Christie dominated the continent throughout his career but it was his ability to step it up and mix it with the best in the world that stood him out from the rest of Britain's sprinters.

His burning desire to be recognised as one of the very best in the world was unrelenting.

Christie now coaches some of the most prestigious talents in the world passing on his pearls of wisdom in the process.

Did you know?
- In 1993, the year after his Olympic success, Christie had an athletics track in West London named after him
- Christie is the only British athlete to have won gold medals in the 100m at all four major competitions and was the first European to run sub-ten seconds
- As a coach, he has overseen the medal winning careers of both Darren Campbell and Katherine Merry

Alphanso Cunningham

Born: Jamaica

Place of birth: August 29, 1980

Sports men and women have on many occasions been dubbed inspirational. Wheelchair-bound Alphanso Cunningham deserves the moniker more than most.

After competing in two Olympics, Paralympian Cunningham, born with a bone deformity in his legs which makes them brittle and unable to support his body, has two gold medals to his name.

Cunningham, nicknamed Anancy, won the discus gold in Athens in 2004 and followed that feat up eight years later when he struck gold at the London 2012 Games via his first place in the javelin.

His achievements have led to the Jamaica Paralympic Association to proudly say on its website: "Also a wheelchair basketball athlete with distinction, Alphanso has been there, done it and continues to do it with supreme authority.'

The deserved plaudits don't end there either. The respected Babsy Grange, Jamaica's opposition spokesperson on Youth, Sports & Culture, has compelled her island's corporate world to back Cunningham and their other Paralympians.

Grange has also called on the entire nation to continue supporting the likes of Cunningham and encourage them as they defy the odds.

Cunningham's London success might not have garnered the same column inches as compatriot Usain Bolt but his success in the English capital were just as noteworthy, if not more so.

Music lover Cunningham threw the javelin a record distance to further excite the legion of Jamaican and Caribbean support that had descended on the greatest show on earth.

Cunningham, who was in third place at the time, surprised his fellow competitors by throwing a regional record of 21.84 metres on his fifth and penultimate throw in the men's 52-53 javelin final.

His London triumph marked Cunningham's second gold medal at the Paralympic Games, having won the discus at the 2004 Athens Games with a world record throw. Coached by Errol Williams, Cunningham is keen that other Jamaican Paralympians get their chance.

The London Games winner says there are Paralympians across the island that have expressed interest in training for international events, but they are unable to travel regularly to the island's capital.

There is just one training centre in Kingston and the lack of facilities could, long term, prove to be a hindrance for those attempting to follow Cunningham's stunning example.

Did You Know?

- In 2012 he was named the Most Outstanding Male Athlete with a Disability at the 2012 Commonwealth Sports Awards gala.
- Cunningham is already looking forward to the next Olympics to be staged in Rio de Janeiro, Brazil. In 2016. He told the Jamaica Star Online: "I will definitely be in Rio, because the discus is closest to my heart."
- Jamaican Prime Minister, Portia Simpson Miller, once said of Cunningham's glittering career: "He has consistently shown that disability is not an obstacle to success.

Jeffrey Dujon

Born: May 28, 1956

Place of Birth: Kingston

When Dujon put on the West Indies wicketkeeper's gloves there were some observers that doubted his credentials. After all the fresh faced cricketer was replacing Deryck Murray who proved so pivotal to the all-conquering Caribbean outfit for years. However, Dujon proved to be up to the task.

He was to make his Test debut against Australia on Boxing Day 1981 and almost a decade later, on August 8, 1991 against England, he was to hang up his international gloves. Surprisingly with one with so much talent, Dujon's only other representative side was Jamaica.

When asked by Telegraph India which West Indies quick bowler really tested him, Dujon replied: "Colin Croft! He had an awkward action and it seemed that everything would go down the leg-side. Mentally, I'd prepare myself for conceding some byes off Croft.

"He was kind of wild, unlike the others. It can get frustrating when things aren't in your control, for the scorecard will show byes and that's a discredit for the keeper."

Dujon's athleticism was key during 81 Tests and 169 one-day internationals, as he kept wicket to some of the fastest bowlers on the planet and did so in some style. Most Tests saw the nimble wicketkeeper flying through the air with the greatest of ease.

Dujon's ability is underpinned by the simple fact that while he was essentially in the West Indies team to snare wickets, his runs were a bonus.

He ranks fifth on the list of most dismissals by wicket keeper in Tests. Only South Africa's Mark Boucher, and Australian trio Adam Gilchrist, Ian Healy and Rodney Marsh top Dujon's 270 dismissals (265 catches and 5 stumpings).

Like his predecessor, Dujon could also handle a bat adequately. He clearly favoured Australia's bowlers, scoring some 1,176 Test runs against the side from Down Under in 23 matches. In total Dujon, who had a swashbuckling sytle about him, scored five Test centuries averaging a highly respectable 31.94.

When Dujon did call time on his career he followed the path of some of those he played with by moving into the media.

Did you know?
- Dujon was named as one of five Wisden Cricketers of the Year in 1989
- With the West Indies having a penchant for fast bowling during his career, Dujon executed just five stumpings during his Test career
- Dujon once gave this piece of advice to those aspiring a career behind the stumps: "A keeper must accept that he can't be perfect and that mistakes will be made."

Debbie Dunn

Born: March 26, 1976

Place of Birth: St Ann

The epitome of an independent woman, Debbie Dunn made the decision to move to the United States, from her Jamaican home, at just 13 years old, showing the commitment, sacrifice and disciplined attitude she has personified throughout her career.

First attempting track and field at Walkers Wood All-Age in St. Ann, she left behind her mother, three brothers and a sister, to join her father in the US, where she blossomed into a world-class 400m runner. However, her path to stardom had many bumps along the way.

In the aftermath of not qualifying to make the 2000 Olympic Games squad, failing to even make the final of the Jamaica national trials, she consciously took time off before deciding to give athletics one last shot.

Showing her famed resilience and grit, she returned to the artificial turf in 2003 but this time with the blazened 'USA' upon her chest, having successfully gained American citizenship.

Still a proud Jamaican, she accepted the support that the USA could provide, in order to give herself the best chance of reaching her potential.

However, Dunn needed time to develop as a senior athlete, despite the excellence she displayed at Norfolk State University, where she became an All-American on numerous occasions and she knew 'she still had it' running a personal best of 49.95 seconds to reach a the 400m final at the 2009 World Championships.

Later, she was celebrating again as a member of the USA 4x400m relay team, outpacing her opponents and landing her first gold medal at a major athletics championship, alongside teammates Allyson Felix, Lashinda Demus and Sanya Richards.

At last the talent she had showed as a student-athlete was being realised as a top-class performer and this was underlined at the 2010 World Indoor Championships in Doha as Dunn achieved her first major individual victory, becoming the 400m queen.

Did you know?
- Dunn's nickname is 'Jackie'
- In a newspaper interview Dunn suggested that she chose to join Norfolk State University because their school colours are predominately green and gold similar to Jamaica's.

Patrick Ewing

Born: August 5, 1962

Place of birth: Kingston

It is to the nation's enduring pride that a son of Jamaica is one of the most recognisable faces in NBA history.

Patrick Ewing was a typical football and cricket-loving West Indian child before making his name in America and beyond.

The 12-year-old left Jamaica to join his family in Cambridge, Massachusetts in 1975 and started playing basketball at school.

His aptitude for his new discipline grew immeasurably and he embarked upon college basketball at Georgetown University in Washington DC.

During his matriculation the Georgetown Hoyas reached the NCAA championship game in three out of four years, with the Hoyas taking the title in 1983-84.

Ewing was building a fine reputation as a centre and added a gold medal to his collection with the USA at the 1984 Los Angeles Olympics.

Ewing was the most sought after player ahead of the 1985 NBA draft and so the authorities were forced to introduce their first-ever Draft Lottery, as the worst placed team were set to get first refusal on Ewing and there were fears that some franchises would deliberately lose matches.

The lottery winners were the New York Knicks for whom the centre would pull on the vest a franchise-record 1,039 times.

Injuries blighted his rookie season but Ewing still made his seven-foot presence felt as he picked up the NBA Rookie of the Year award.

He was an integral part of the original US 'Dream Team' at the 1992 Barcelona Olympics, when active NBA players were first permitted to represent the USA.

Ewing, alongside such illustrious names such as Michael Jordan, Magic Johnson and Larry Bird, comprised one of the most dominant sporting teams in history during their strident march to gold.

Though Ewing's performances throughout his Knicks career were imperious the NBA title eluded him in an era when Jordan's dominant Chicago Bulls won three in a row.

When New York finally overcame their temporarily Jordan-less Chicago adversaries in the 1994 Eastern Conference play-off semi-finals they went on to reach the NBA finals only to lose out to the Houston Rockets, having lost in the final seconds of games six and seven.

Ewing left for the Seattle Supersonics in 2000 and in 2001-02 played his final season at Orlando Magic, whom he has gone on to coach as an assistant.

In 2003 New York retired his number 33 vest in recognition of the achievements of the finest player in their history.

Did you know?
- Ewing is an 11-times NBA All-Star
- He scored 24,815 NBA points at an average of 21.0 points per game
- In 2010 he coached his son Patrick Jr when he represented Orlando.

Brigitte Foster-Hylton

Born: November 7, 1974

Place of Birth: St Elizabeth

As hurdlers go, there are not many who can match the glorious accomplishments of Foster-Hylton in her long and esteemed career as one of Jamaica's greatest females to glide over the 100m stretch.

Notable for her hysterical leaping celebration in response to storming her way to a long awaited gold medal at the World Championships in 2009, Foster-Hylton stooped furthest to beat Beijing Olympic bronze medallist Priscilla Lopes-Schliep and compatriot Delloreen Ennis-London.

It followed up on her gallantly won World Championship silver and bronze medals from the two previous World Championships in Helsinki and Paris, respectively.

Then Jamaican Prime Minister, Bruce Golding, presented the evergreen performer with the Courtney Walsh Award for Excellence in 2009, becom-

ing only the fifth recipient of the crystal ball recognising her outstanding achievements.

Charming both in personality and performance, Foster-Hylton's career began to come to the fore in 2000 when she took 65/100th of a second off her personal best, before reaching an Olympic 100m hurdle final later the same year in Sydney.

Only six years later, back in Australia she blew away the field to record her first gold medal in a major championship at the 2006 Commonwealth Games.

Off the track, she is married to Patrick Hylton, Group Managing Director of National Commercial Bank in Jamaica.

Unfortunately, she crashed out of the heats at London 2012, following her tumble over the fifth hurdle whilst leading the field, sparking understandably heartbroken yelps of emotion in front of the world's cameras.

The second fastest woman on earth, despite much of her competition being 10-15 years her junior, she knew she was in great shape to clinch that long awaited Olympic gold, but it wasn't to be.

Despite her plethora of medals, her biggest feats are probably off the track, whereby her hard-work, determination and drive has made her a firm fans favourite influencing both men and, in particular, women, to delve through the back pages of newspapers.

Thus, her global appeal and her mental rigidity to fight against major injuries and subsequent surgery has gained her the type of respect in her homeland that will live long in the hearts of the locals.

Did You Know?
- Foster-Hylton has a bachelor's degree in Speech Communications
- The popular sprint hurdler has won the Jamaican Sportswoman of the Year three times; 2002, 2003 and 2009.

Shelly-Ann Fraser-Pryce

Born: December 27, 1986

Place of birth: Kingston

It isn't every day that an Olympic and world champion declares that there is still much more to come.

In early August 2013, the highly decorated Jamaican sprinter told her rivals that they had better watch out as she still has much to do in the 100m, 200m and sprint relay.

She was as good as her word when she added World Championship 100m, 200m and 4x100m relay gold to her already impressive collection.

Before the World Championships, held in Moscow, she told The Voice newspaper: "There are no limits to my potential. There are sometimes things I want to say [in terms of future ambitions] but I like to relax and let things flow naturally."

The London 2012 100m gold medallist added: "I believe that I am going to be one of the greatest athletes of all time. Everybody wants to win Olympic and world gold - but I also want to be amongst the greats.

"I want to go where no female athlete has gone before, I want to win three Olympic gold medals – I even want to break the world record. The best of Shelly-Ann Fraser-Pryce is yet to come!

"I won't limit myself. God has given me the strength to conquer anything. The only thing I have to do is put in the work. I am putting in that work as I know nothing comes easy."

In 2008 she announced herself to the world at the Beijing Olympics - and in some style.

The gifted Jamaican stormed to 100m glory becoming the first Caribbean woman to win the short sprint at the Olympics.

The diminutive Fraser-Pryce's infectious smile temporarily disappeared in 2010 when she had to serve a six-month ban from athletics after a urine

sample taken at the 2010 Shanghai Diamond League meeting was found to contain a banned narcotic Oxycodone.

The committed Christian is grateful that her faith and family remained steadfast.

She said: "Having the right people in your corner definitely helps; having the right support system is crucial because things can get tough.

"There are days when you are tired, sick, injured or fed up but the support around you helps and I am privileged to have a blessed family.

"My faith is also very important because there is only one person I trust and that is God because he has never ever failed me. I always try and find joy in everything that I do.

"If I was to leave athletics now I would be happy and pleased with what I have already accomplished. I will continue to be grounded and stay humble."

Did You Know?
- The athlete is an ambassador for Grace Foods
- In January 2011 she married long-term boyfriend Jason Pryce

Ricardo Gardner

Born: September 25, 1978
Place of Birth: St. Andrew

When the history of Jamaican footballers is reviewed Gardner's chapter will prove to be highly significant.

The defender, who made his name at left-back, sprung to prominence at the 1998 World Cup in France where he starred for the Reggae Boyz at their first ever finals.

Nicknamed 'Bibi' by those close to him, Gardner's consistent displays at the ultimate football showcase earned him a £1 million transfer from his local Harbour View club to Bolton just month later. He went on to be good value.

Gardner's move was to open the door for dozens more as players from Jamaica, and the rest of the Caribbean, frequently headed to big name European clubs as young men targeted lucrative contracts abroad. His contribution to the game, with next to little fanfare, can only be described as immense. Pioneer is an often used word but that is exactly what Gardner has been.

The diminutive defender, whose versatility made him key to Bolton's rise and rise, suffered numerous career-threatening injuries during his career but showed mental toughness to go with his on field doggedness.

He appeared over 400 times for Bolton developing into a genuine fans' favourite along the way.

Among Gardner's club highlights came when he scored his first goal at club level in nearly five years when he opened the scoring in Bolton's 2-2 draw against German giants Bayern Munich at the Allianz Arena in a UEFA Cup match in 2007.

Gardner, who gained 109 international caps, left Bolton Wanderers in May 2012. The Lancashire club were relegated from the Premier League to

the Championship and the utility player was one of a dozen players subsequently released.

The Jamaican had not been included in Bolton's squad of 25 players for the second half of the season, fuelling speculation that his 14 year career at the club would soon come to an end. After being initially sidelined with a thigh strain it was discovered that Gardner had also suffered another knee injury.

Bolton manager at the time, Owen Coyle, said of Gardner: "He has offered incredible service to Bolton and I'd like to personally thank him for all of his efforts, particularly during the time I have worked with him."

In May 2013, after spending the better part of 15 years on English soil, the majority with Bolton Wanderers, Gardner returned to Jamaica.

Did You Know?

- In 2006, Gardner was named Bolton's Player of the Year
- The left-back had a four match loan spell with Preston North End in 2011
- Gardner is 5 feet 9 inches tall

Chris Gayle

Born: September 21, 1979
Place of birth: Kingston

Chris Gayle, like the legend that is Sir Vivian Richards, has gained his reputation by being a big-hitting batsman who has a liking for treating bowlers – fast or slow – with total disdain.

His highest score in the ultimate format of the game is 333, which he achieved in a Test against New Zealand in 2010. His incredible innings contained nine sixes and 34 boundaries in his 437-ball knock.

But it is in one-day cricket, and in the Twenty20 version especially, that Gayle has proved to be a genuine force.

Gayle was present and correct as the Allen Stanford-inspired Superstars, during a match that globally and controversially introduced the T20 format to the world, crushed England by 10 wickets in November 2008.

Chasing a score of 99, Gayle notched a dominant 65 not out off 45 deliveries. His strong liking for T20, the shortest format of the game, had been cast.

His ability to endanger the figures of most bowlers – and the wellbeing of those sitting in the stands with his big hitting – has made Gayle a fortune as he carried his bat around the world.

Gayle confirmed his status as an outstanding limited overs batsman in April 2013.

The Jamaican, while playing for Royal Challengers Bangalore recorded the highest individual total by a batsman in cricket's T20 format. Off just 66 balls, Gayle scored 175 runs, smashing the previous best T20 score of 158 by New Zealander Brendon McCullum.

Furthermore, the West Indian also racked up the fastest century in cricket's history off just 30 balls playing for the Royal Challengers Bangalore in the T20 Indian Premier League (IPL).

Gayle's career was tainted by his much chronicled and high profile dispute with the West Indies Cricket Board. He was to earn a recall to the West Indies squad for the one-day series against England in 2012, bringing an end to a 14-month exile for the former captain.

While he has set the limted overs format alight, Gayle said in August 2013 that he feels "sad" when people overlook what he has achieved in Test cricket.

The crowd pleaser admitted that he does not like when his career in the traditional form of the sport to be neglected. He told *The Indian Express*: "I have been giving my all for West Indies for 13 years now. "So it's sad when people just forget all that I've achieved for the Caribbean and use such derogatory terms.

"I have scored runs and won matches in Test cricket as well. There are other cricketers too who get bracketed in that category. It's unfair but you can't stop tongues from wagging."

Did You Know?
- Football-mad Gayle is a Manchester United supporter
- For one-day internationals for West Indies, Gayle plays in the no.45 shirt

George Headley

Born: May 30, 1909 – November 30, 1983
Place of birth: Colon, Panama

Forever linked to Jamaica, George Headley carried a West Indies cricket team long before that burden fell on Brian Lara's shoulders. The man who became known as the 'black Bradman' was the sole world class talent in the West Indies side of the 1930s.

The medium built number three often had the Test side's success hinging on his performances. During 22 Tests he scored 2,190 runs, including 10 centuries, and was the first man to score centuries in both innings of a Test at Lord's.

Headley was actually born in Panama where his Barbadian father worked in the construction of the canal. He was taken to his mother's homeland of Jamaica when he was 10 in order to perfect his English. It was also hoped that he would eventually study dentistry in America.

That avenue finally closed when he excelled during a match against a touring English side in 1928. The 18-year-old Headley was only able to participate due to a delay in obtaining his passport for America. Dentistry's loss was cricket's gain.

The right-hander was overlooked for the West Indies 1928 tour of England but was selected when the English toured the Caribbean in 1929-30.

He scored 708 runs in eight Test innings and averaged 87.80 during the series and posted equally impressive figures on the West Indies tour of Australia in 1930-31 when he claimed two centuries and ended the tour with 1,066 runs.

When in 1933 Headley went to England to play for Haslington in the Lancashire League special dispensation was granted for him to continue playing for the West Indies.

The nimble-footed Headley was renowned for his stroke play on the on-side and had a knack for using his superb play off the back foot to evade fielders with his precise shot-making.

It was also said that he never rushed a shot and he certainly bought poise to an erratic batting line-up in the days before the West Indies became a world power.

Headley was not quite the same force when first-class cricket resumed after the Second World War although he was selected to captain the West Indies against England for one Test in 1948.

The politics of the time would not allow a black player to hold the captaincy on a permanent basis.

Headley died in Kingston on November 30, 1983, aged 74, having set the standards by which future generations of Caribbean cricketers would be judged.

Did you know?

- His son Ron was an opening bat for Worcestershire and Derbyshire and played twice for the West Indies against England. His grandson Dean played Test cricket for England
- Headley was chosen as one of the Wisden Cricketers of the Year in 1933

Deon Hemmings

Born: September 10, 1968

Place of Birth: St Ann

Legend and pioneer are two terms somewhat overused in describing modern day sports men and women but when applied to Deon Hemmings, they are clearly a severe understatement.

For Hemmings was the first Jamaican woman to win an Olympic gold medal in the 400m hurdles when she stormed down the back straight to reign supreme in the 1996 Atlanta Olympic Games, setting a brand new Olympic record which had stood for eight years.

The leggy St Ann native followed up her outstanding display in the following Olympics in the millennium in sun-glazed Sydney, picking up two silver medals in her natural discipline the 400m, and the 4x400m relay, teamed with Sandie Richards, Catherine Scott-Pomales and Lorraine Graham.

All of this was achieved by the energetic Hemmings despite a relatively unspectacular high school athletics career at York Castle High School and Vere Technical High School, but suddenly she began to find her golden pathway to track and field form while ascending through the ranks of 400m hurdles at Central Ohio State University, before reaching her first major championships, the Barcelona Olympics of 1992.

In her next major competition, the 1994 Commonwealth Games in Victoria, Canada, Hemmings surprised many with a second place finish and subsequent silver medal.

This was followed by another silver medal in the 1997 World Championships, sandwiched between claiming a bronze in both the 1995 and 1999 world extravaganzas.

Apart from her stellar sporting career her humble and modest mannerism appeals to many in and outside of Jamaica, as well as her desire to avoid

the superstar status, she purveys a sense of realism; juggling motherhood and her job as an estate agent.

Did you know?
- Hemmings married Michael McCatty in 2004, a year after retiring from competitive track and field
- The one-lap specialist ran an IAAF Kids Clinic in Kingston, Jamaica, on the eve of the IAAF/Coca Cola World Junior Championships which was the first IAAF World Athletic Series competition to be held in Jamaica
- Hemmings studied business administration at Central State University, Ohio

Michael Holding

Born: February 16, 1954

Place of birth: Half Way Tree, Kingston

The stunning career of Michael Holding owes much to the West Indies painful visit to Australia in 1975. It was that pivotal tour of duty Down Under that compelled Holding to grow up quickly as he and his team mates were devoured by fast bowlers Jeff Thomson and Dennis Lillee.

Legend has it that Holding was reduced to tears but like the rest of his team mates, who included Clive Lloyd and Vivian Richards, he vowed to never be dismantled like that again.

One of the fastest bowlers to play Test cricket, Holding was to go on to terrorise many a batsman himself. He was to take 249 wickets in 60 Tests and 142 wickets in 102 one-day internationals as he lived up to his moniker of 'Whispering Death' such was his quiet approach to the bowling crease.

His unique run-up was best illustrated at the famous Oval ground in 1976. The graceful Holding took 14 wickets for 149 in the Oval Test against England, the finest match figures ever by a West Indian.

The lithe Holding, who cut his teeth at the famous Melbourne Cricket Club in his homeland, had many outstanding matches as he formed an awesome West Indies pace quartet which at different times included Andy Roberts, Malcolm Marshall, Joel Garner, Sylvester Clarke, Colin Croft and Wayne Daniel. The group were to forever change West Indies fortunes in the international game and set a template that others would follow.

What made Holding great amongst those bowling luminaries was his pace of delivery. He was arguably the quickest of them all, and would defeat batsman with sheer speed, and incredible accuracy.

A review of the long history of West Indies fast bowlers has Holding just behind Malcolm Marshall, Curtly Ambrose and Joel Garner in the eyes of many observers. But Holding has his supporters and in vast numbers.

His outstanding career also saw him play for his native Jamaica, Tasmania and Lancashire, Derbyshire and Canterbury in the United Kingdom.

Holding made a seamless move into the media after retirement. His excellent commentary on Sky Sports has proved to be insightful and popular.

Did you know?

- In June 1988 Holding was celebrated on the $2 Jamaican stamp
- Holding loves his horse racing, has a home in Newmarket and a share in a horse, Vallani, trained by Walter Swinburn
- Despite a batting average of 13.78, Holding holds the record for the most sixes (36) in a Test career for any player with fewer than 1,000 career runs

Jackie Hendriks

Born: December 21, 1933

Place of birth: St Andrew

Jackie Hendriks' name is central to any debate on the greatest wicketkeepers in West Indies history.

The tall and affable Hendriks, from St Andrew in Kingston, vied with a youthful Deryck Murray throughout the 1960s to keep wicket in a West Indies side that was set to dominate Test cricket.

Hendriks, a future coach, match referee and administrator, was a gifted glovesman who was reliable whether standing up or back.

He made his Test debut against India in Port of Spain in February 1962 and topped scored with 64 in the Windies' first innings despite sustaining a broken finger.

He took a catch in the same match and it seemed a promising start for the 28-year-old as he sought to fill the gloves of the retired Gerry Alexander. Yet Hendriks would not put on the maroon cap in the Test arena for another three years, as Trinidad's precocious Deryck Murray was handed his opportunity and seized it with aplomb.

He returned to the Test side to face Australia on home territory in the first Test at Sabina Park in Kingston in 1965.

Hendriks was performing an integral role in the Windies' 2-1 series victory when a Graham McKenzie bouncer hospitalised him during the fourth Test in Bridgetown.

His life was in the balance for a time but he made a full recovery and went on to play a further 15 Tests, all in series overseas.

He played only 20 Tests in total, restricted as he was by the form of Murray, his own injuries, as was the case when England toured the Caribbean in 1967-68, and the fact that Test schedules were not so heavily loaded as they are in the present era. Nonetheless he took 42 catches and five

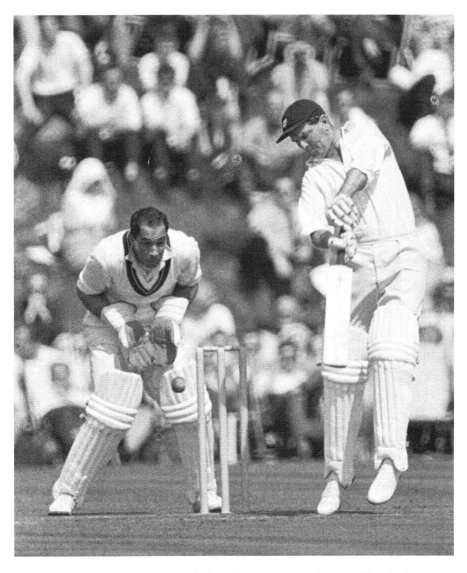

stumpings in those Tests. With his Test average of 18.62 Hendriks was a modest batsmen and not so well-rounded a player as stylish Jeff Dujon, but Guyanese pace bowling legend Colin

Croft felt Hendriks was the 'purest' wicket-keeper in West Indies history.

"It should also be noted that he is perhaps the last West Indian wicket-keeper to have been behind the stumps for a properly varied bowling attack," wrote Croft for Cricinfo in 1999.

"As he had to cope with Wes Hall, Charlie Griffith and the rest of the fast bowlers, along with the leg-spin of Gary Sobers and off-spin of Lance Gibbs, among others, that, more than anything else, makes him stand out."

Did you know?

- In 1988 Hendriks appeared on the 25 cent Jamaican stamp alongside the Barbados Cricket Buckle
- He three times kept without conceding a bye in totals that exceeded 500 runs
- Hendriks attended Wolmer's School in Kingston, which has produced six Test wicket-keepers: Karl Nunes, Ivan Barrow, Gerry Alexander, Hendriks, Jeff Dujon and Carlton Baugh

Bunny Johnson

Born: May 10, 1947

Place of birth: Kingston

Bunny Johnson was one of the first Jamaican immigrants to leave his mark on British sport.

Johnson came to England at 16 to join his dad, who was a car worker, and his mum, a machinist. Within 12 years the ambitious pugilist was the British and Commonwealth heavyweight champion and became an inspiration to all second generation West Indians in the UK.

When the teenage Johnson arrived in England he faced a choice between pursuing his interest in law, which he nurtured back home by reading various books on English law and famous British trials, or taking his chances as a boxer.

His biggest sporting inspiration as a child was his famous American namesake Jack Johnson.

After a glittering 13-year ring career it is not one Johnson regrets but perhaps it was not the most obvious choice for the bookish adolescent.

"I was not really good at anything sporting-wise, not to compete rigorously, anyway," he told journalist Ernest Cashmore in 1979. "I wasn't an outstanding athlete and had more of an interest in reading."

Nonetheless, the youngster trained vigorously and made his professional debut in 1968, knocking out Peter Thomas in the second round.

He steadily built his reputation and many observers declared that Johnson had the hardest pound-for-pound left hook in the British fight game at that time.

By early 1975 Johnson was eligible to fight for the British title under the 10-year residency rule.

On January 13 he knocked out Danny McAlinden in the ninth round at Grosvenor

House in Mayfair in central London to become the first immigrant to claim the British and Commonwealth heavyweight titles.

However, in September of the same year he lost both titles in his first defence to long-term rival Richard Dunn.

Defeat caused Johnson to acknowledge that he was more suited to the light-heavyweight division.

He duly claimed the British light-heavyweight title on March 8, 1977 with a first-round knockout of Tim Wood in Wolverhampton.

Though Johnson was stopped in the 11th round when he met Aldo Traversaro for the vacant European light-heavyweight title the following November he won the Lonsdale belt outright in 1979 with two successful defences of his British title against Harry White and Rab Affleck. He added a third with a points decision over Dennis Andries in February 1980.

Johnson retired with a record of 73 fights, 55 victories (33 knockouts), 17 defeats and one draw.

Did you know?

- Johnson has a seat on the Midlands Boxing Council
- He is also president of the Central Ex-Boxers Association, a charity that helps retired Midlands boxers who have fallen on hard times;
- Johnson is a police station representative who predominantly works with young offenders.

Glencoffe Johnson

Born: January 2, 1969

Place of birth: Clarendon

Glencoffe Johnson was once described "as the boxer that will never go away." Known perversely as the 'Road Warrior' or 'The Gentelman' Johnson was a throwback to the time when men entered the ring to fight and do away with show boating.

Johnson usually fought as the underdog but his classy ring displays and massive heart would see him win the plaudits in the end.

One such instance came about in September 2004 when one of the sport's true icons, Roy Jones, Jr, hand picked him as an opponent and paid for it. A crunching right hand sent Jones to the floor, out cold and placed Johnson into the big league by claiming the IBF version of the heavyweight crown.

He followed up with another upset win over Antonio Tarver (to win the IBO light-heavyweight title), he held his own with Chad Dawson and Tavoris Cloud, and has proven to be one of the most durable men in boxing a pastime deemed one of the toughest in the world.

But Johnson admits that beating Briton Clinton Woods in September 2006, aged 37, for the IBF light-heavyweight crown is his proudest moment.

As well as being tenacious, Johnson appeared to defy Father Time. He was still be putting up a good fight against younger men into his early 40s as was displayed when he lost a unanimous points decision against the highly regarded Romanian-Canadian Lucian Bute in November 2011 in Quebec, Canada. The judges scorecards read 119-109 and 120-108 twice to confirm that Johnson had given it, yet again, his best shot against the odds.

Johnson was still fighting up until April 2013 and proving to be a winner when he beat Junior Ramos from the Dominican Republic by TKO in the second round of their bout.

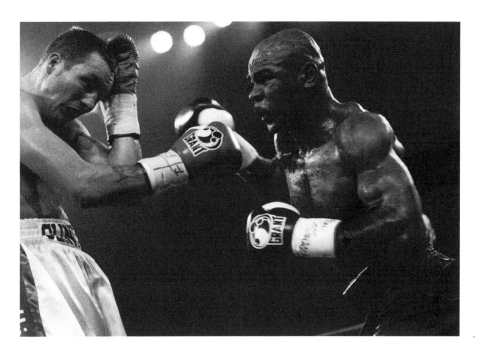

When asked about his longevity in the hardest profession of all, Johnson said in July 2012: "I like the challenge. I'm excited about going out there and doing the things I do. People are still excited about seeing me perform. Mostly, I keep doing it because I'm still enjoying it."

That philosophy summed up Glencoffe Johnson as a man and as a fighter; humble and effective at the same time. There might have been more significant talents to grace the ring but not too many would have drawn greater admiration

Did You Know?

- Johnson is a diehard Miami heat basketball fan
- Muhammad Ali, Roy Jones Jr., Evander Holyfield and Mike Tyson are all listed as idols by Johnson
- Johnson has admitted that Bernard Hopkins was his toughest opponent

Mike McCallum

Born: December 7, 1956

Place of Birth: Kingston

Nicknames are among the subjects that make sport exciting. However, one cannot be more apt than Mike McCallum's 'Body Snatcher.'

McCallum attacked the midsections of his opponents like no other pugilist as he carved out a career that saw him win major titles in three weight classes; junior-middleweight, middleweight and light-heavyweight.

The Jamaican was the first from his sports mad island to win a major boxing title when he beat Sean Mannion over 15 rounds in 1981 to secure the junior-middleweight World Boxing Association (WBA) crown.

McCallum's fearsome reputation meant that the very best avoided him during the 1980s. The highly respected The Ring magazine hit the nail on the head when it said that McCallum 'was unable to coax the Big Four – Roberto Duran, Thomas Hearns, Marvin Hagler or Sugar Ray Leonard – into the ring.' A bout against either of that quartet would have been a must-see event.

McCallum was destined for great things from the outset of his career as an amateur. At the age of just 20, he secured a berth in the 1976 Jamaica Olympic team which competed in Montreal, Canada.

He was to turn professional on February 19, 1981 and saw off Mannion just months later. But the best was yet to come. McCallum proved his class with wins over some of boxing's best as he defended his WBA belt six times.

McCallum proved too much for the likes of Julian Jackson, Milton McCrory and the highly-rated Donald Curry. He added the WBA middle-weight crown to his burgeoning CV with a win over Briton Herol 'Bomber' Graham in 1989 before completing his hat-trick with a win over Jeff Harding to land the WBC light-heavyweight belt. McCallum retired in 1997

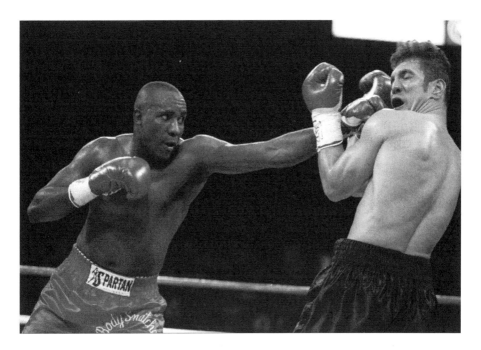

with a 49-5-1 (36) record. Observers marked him down as a great techni-
cian within the ropes. Fittingly, on retirement McCallum went on to be a
trainer in Las Vegas.

Did you know?

- McCallum was inducted into the International Boxing Hall of Fame
  in 2003
- The Jamaican pugilist was never knocked out as a professional
- For his outstanding career, McCallum was recognised when he
  received an award at the Caribbean Awards for Sports Icons (CASI) in
  his native Jamaica

Herb McKenley

Born: July 10, 1922 – November 26, 2007
Place of Birth: Pleasant Valley, Clarendon

"Once I'm in the lead at the top of the home stretch, no man in the world can beat me," McKenley once said, and he was right. A larger-than-life figure, and former fastest 400m runner on the planet, McKenley was a pioneering figure who led the way for the Jamaican track and field stars of today.

Breaking his old world record of 46.3 seconds in the 440 yard sprint in 1947, with an outstanding time of 46 seconds flat just a year later, adding to the then-feat of achieving the fastest time ever in the 400 metres – the New York Times called him 'The man who couldn't be beaten'.

A born-winner, McKenley got his hands on Olympic gold at Helsinki 1952 in the 4x400m relay, where he transformed a 10-yard deficit into a healthy lead with an exhilarating leg of 44.6 seconds, adding to his two silvers in the 100m and his standard event, the 400m.

His father, a doctor, McKenley's mother wanted him to be a violinist, thus sent him, aged 12, to lessons more than two and a half miles away from the family home – but instead of getting transport, he ran.

As a youngster, he was running 51.6 seconds at high school and eventually became the first Jamaican sprinter to receive a college scholarship in the United States, successfully attending Boston College in 1942 before moving to the University of Illinois.

The significance of this on Jamaican society, not merely national athletes, can never be overestimated as now between 60 to 100 Jamaican boys and girls are on a U.S.A scholarship each year.

After a variety of health problems, including triple bypass surgery in 1998, McKenley died due to complications with a bout of pneumonia in Kingston, Jamaica, aged 85.

McKenley had served as both national coach and latterly, as president of Jamaica's Amateur Athletic Association, where he was instrumental in leading a youth athletics programme which produced global superstars such as Don Quarrie and Lennox Miller.

Did you know?

- August 23, 1947, on a wind-aided straight boardwalk at Long Branch, New Jersey, McKenley was timed in 45 seconds for 440 yards, a claimant to being the first person to break the 45 second barrier at 400 metres.

- At the first 1951 Pan-American Games in Buenos Aires, McKenley was third in the 100m, 200m and 400m, the only person to ever perform this feat.

- McKenley was appointed to the Jamaican Order of Merit in 2004

Marilyn Neufville

Born: November 16, 1952
Place of birth: Portland, Jamaica

The Diminutive Marilyn Neufville certainly created big headlines in 1970.

Born in Jamaica, Neufville had emigrated aged eight to Great Britain.

Neufville, now residing in the UK, cannot have imagined what controversy she would have created in 1970 when she decided to represent Jamaica in the Commonwealth Games in Edinburgh when wearing an international athletic vest.

The 400m runner was shown little tolerance by a dismayed British public and she was left in little doubt that her decision was an unpopular one in many quarters.

She was subsequently a subject for media and British athletics officials angst who wanted to know exactly why she had come to her contentious decision.

Her troubles had arisen because just after her 17th birthday, in March 1970, the Jamaican had proudly represented Great Britain at the European Indoor Championships in Vienna, where she won the 400m in 53.01sec.

But she was to turn her back on GB just months later.

The Commonwealth Games in Scotland saw Neufville show her undoubted class. The 5' 5" one lap exponent established a new world record at the tender age of just 17.

However, her career would be blighted by injury, often having to undergo surgery. Some observers pointed to her slight frame as leading to her regular physical break down. Add the political pressures she was also under, and her career had little chance for growth.

She also competed at the 1974 Commonwealth Games but was a mere shadow of her former self only finishing sixth in the 400m final.

In the 1976 Summer Olympics Neufville made her Olympic debut finishing fourth in her heat but had to pull out of her round 2 heat through injury.

This gifted athlete had first come to attention of the media and public in 1967 she won two Amateur Athletic Association (AAA) of England sprint titles in the under-15 group: the 100 and 150 yards (in 17.3 seconds).

After her athletics career, Neufville took up employment in the USA and UK as a social worker.

Did You Know…?

- Neufville won the Jamaica Sportswoman of the year awards in 1970 and 1971
- She was a member of Cambridge Harriers

Merlene Ottey

Born: May 10, 1960

Place of Birth: Cold Spring, Hanover

Beautiful, majestic and endearing, few athletes, if any, will ever achieve what sprint queen Merlene Ottey has in track and field.

Even aged 52 years young, Ottey was still making headlines in 2012 by attempting to qualify for her eighth Olympic Games.

Add to that her inclusion in the Slovenia team (her adopted home since 1998) that went to Helsinki for the European Championships, making her the oldest ever participant in that competition, and you begin to understand that Ottey has done what few are able to, turned the art of sprinting into a marathon.

Ottey's career started to take shape in 1979 where a spindly sprinter rocked up to the Pan American Games with little or no inkling that she would go onto be an integral part of a female sprinting era that has firmly set itself apart from any other in athletics history.

Having competed against the legendary Americans Flo-Jo and Gail Devers at the 1988 and 1992 Olympic Games as well as the much maligned Marion Jones at the Sydney 2000 Games, Ottey can legitimately claim to have seen it all.

Her personal best times over 100m and 200m (10.74s and 21.64s respectively) would put her in the top three of all time even in 2012. Ottey was also the first woman to run the 60m indoors in less than seven seconds.

There are so many records attributed to Ottey it's hard to rank them in terms of their significance.

The durable sprinter also won 73 successive finals from May 1989 to March 1991.

Among the many though, is the fact that Ottey is the oldest Olympic athletics medallist and also holds a record 14 world championship medals, three of them gold.

She was also the first female athlete from the Caribbean to win an Olympic medal, Ottey climbed the Olympic podium for the first time at the 1980 Moscow Games over three decades ago.

Did you know?

- Ottey has won a record nine Olympic medals, the most by any athlete, but none of them has been gold.
- The sprinter is one of only two athletes to win twenty plus medals at the Olympic Games and the World Championships combined, the other is Carl Lewis.
- Ottey holds the record for running the fastest indoor 200m in 21.87 seconds. This record has now stood for 19 years and remains the only sub 22seconds clocking by a woman.

Asafa Powell

Born: November 23, 1982

Place of Birth: Spanish Town, St Catherine, Jamaica

For many years the most prominent 100m sprinter to wear the famous black, green and gold of Jamaica was Asafa Powell, who incidentally has clocked more sprints below-10 seconds than any other athlete in the history of the sport.

Combining a very idiosyncratic tight-running style with explosive leg power, Powell matched his 2002 Commonwealth Games silver medal won as part of the Jamaican 4x100m relay team, in Manchester, with a gold, in the relay and the 100m in the following Commonwealth Games in Melbourne.

To date the third fastest man ever, he has won credible individual 100m bronze medals at the World Championships in Osaka 2007 and Berlin 2009, as well being a member of the 4x100m relay team which destroyed the then world record, with a time of 37.10 seconds while storming to gold. In 2009, he even improved his personal best time, recording 9.72 seconds in Lausanne, Switzerland.

A strapping 6' 2", Powell first made the international headlines after running a world record time of 9.77 seconds in the summer of 2005, aptly at the home of athletics, Athens, Greece.

He repeated the feat a year later in Switzerland – ending 2006 with 12 legal sub-10-second clockings.

His rise was of such velocity, that the engineering student had to postpone various stages of his studies at Kingston's University of Technology, as he was regularly in Europe competing in front of thousands of spectators.

Notwithstanding his superstar status, and all the trappings that accompany it, Powell is well known for his humble, soft-spoken nature, ascribing much of that to the influence of his family.

The youngest of six sons, Powell has frequently affirmed his strong relationship with his parents, both church ministers, as instrumental in keeping his feet on the ground.

During high school, Powell didn't produce particularly spectacular track results, but his raw talent impressed the on-looking coach Stephen Francis, representing the MVP Track club, who has steered his career since 2001.

A failed drugs test in 2013 however, has taken some of the gloss off of the aura that surrounded Powell.

Having tested positive for the banned stimulant oxilofrine at the Jamaican Championships that year, the debate surrounding the validity of his legacy will ensue forever.

Did you know?

- In the seven year history of the IAAF World Athletics Final (2003–2009), Powell won the most competitions of any male athlete and took home the most prize money in the male events. In his seven appearances at the competition, he won the 100m four times and the 200m once, winning US$173,000 in total.
- Powell was an avid car enthusiast as a child and built his own go-kart which he used to drive around the community.
- Sprinting runs in Powell's family. His eldest brother Donovan, was a 60m finalist in the 1999 World Indoor Championships. For the 100 yard dash, his mother ran 11.4s, and his father 10.2s.

Don Quarrie

Born: February 25, 1951

Place of Birth: Kingston

When names are referred to as being synonymous with a sport then few can be as significant as Donald Riley Quarrie.

The inspiration for so many athletes who have followed, Quarrie attended five Olympic Games for Jamaica and literally put the Caribbean island on the track and field map.

Success for Quarrie wasn't instant, indeed, the first Olympic Games the 17-year-old attended in 1968 ended for him when a freak training incident ruled him out of competing.

It wasn't to be until eight years later that Quarrie would cement his name in sporting history but in the years that preceded the 1976 Montreal Olympic Games Quarrie really made his mark.

At the 1970 Commonwealth Games Quarrie, still only 19 years of age and with everything to do, won the sprint double in the 100m and 200m.

The double success confirmed what so many had known in Jamaica for a while; in no uncertain terms the big secret was out.

The good form Quarrie demonstrated didn't prepare him for the 1972 Munich Olympic Games however, where he missed out on a podium finish.

But the wily competitor still garnered the kind of knowledge that would be integral for him to draw upon if he was to experience future success.

Rolling on four years and the hopes of a nation were firmly resting on Quarrie's shoulders. For the first time in many years there was a genuine gold medal hopeful in the sprints. Quarrie didn't disappoint, claiming the gold in the 100m and the silver in the 200m.

Quarrie followed up those victories two years later at the Edmonton, Canada Commonwealth Games where he won his third consecutive title over 100m.

Quarrie has gone on to use his experience to help Jamaica's talented crop of youngsters.

He was technical leader of the London 2012 Jamaica Olympic team which illiuminated the greatest show on Earth.

Quarrie has imparted his wisdom on the next generation of Olympians in the hope that they can keep the Jamaican winning tradition alive.

Did you know?
- A statue of Quarrie has been erected outside of Jamaica's National Stadium since 1978. The Olympian has also had a school named after him (Donald Quarrie High School) in Eastern Kingston
- In 1971 the athlete broke the world record for the 200m, setting a time of 19.80s at the Pan American Games
- In 1975 Quarrie was awarded the Order of Distinction and in 1998 he was inducted into Jamaica Sports Hall of Fame

Allan Rae

Born: September 30, 1922 – February 27, 2005
Place of birth: Rollington Town, Kingston

How the West Indies Cricket Board (WICB) could now use someone like Allan Rae. The Kingston-born cricketer enjoyed a brief but fruitful Test career as a dogged left-handed opening batsman before entering management and helping to shape the West Indies sides that dominated cricket from the late 1970s through to the early 1990s.

Rae was summoned from his law degree in London to make his Test debut in Delhi in November 1948.

His maiden century (104) followed in the second Test in Bombay and he also posted a knock of 97 back in Delhi for the fifth Test to end the tour with an average of 53.42.

Rae, who played as an amateur, soon struck up his renowned partnership with fellow opener Jeffrey Stollmeyer and the pair brought stability to the West Indies top order for the first time, as their opening stand of 239 in the fourth Test in Madras demonstrated.

The West Indies were no longer a soft touch and the pair built a platform for the youthful trio of Frank Worrell, Clyde Walcott and Everton Weekes to cement their global reputations.

Rae and Stollmeyer presented the first obstacle in an emerging West Indies team that beat a strong England side 3-1 on their 1950 tour, with centuries at Lord's and the Oval helping Rae to finish the tour with an average of 62.83.

England represented the pinnacle. Rae struggled to come to terms with the Australians' pace on the lively pitches of the West Indies' 1951-2 tour and played only six more Tests and retired at 30 to become a barrister.

Yet his relationship with Jamaican and Caribbean cricket was far from over and his involvement in the game often, it was said, impinged upon his work at his law practice.

Rae became president at both the Jamaican and West Indies cricket boards and his skilful administration at the WICB between 1981 and 1988 took in their most successful side.

His diplomatic nous was evident in his sensible accommodation of Australian tycoon Kerry Packer's unofficial World Series, which saw the England and Wales Cricket Board lose an expensive court case.

Rae also drew praise for his stance against the defectors who took part in the 1982-1990 rebel tours of the suspended South Africa.

His death in 2005, aged 82, offered a small reminder of what Caribbean cricket has been missing for so long.

Did you know?

- His father, Ernest Rae, toured England with the West Indies in 1928
- He met King George VI in dirty flannels at Lord's in 1950 after refusing to change. 'I'd rather have the King think I was a dirty man than be out because I was rushing to change.'
- In 1988 his image appeared on the $4 Jamaican stamp alongside the Barbados Cricket Buckle.

Sanya Richards-Ross

Born: February 26, 1985

Place of birth: Kingston

Not many sprinters can look as glamorous as the Kingston-born USA 400m sprinter Sanya Richards-Ross, whose calm, patience and confidence led her to finally get her hands around her long awaited Olympic gold individual medal at London 2012.

Following the disappointment of failing to win a gold in Beijing, her courage, determination and resilience lifted her to avenge those past sorrows.

Incredibly successful in the 4x400m relays, winning gold in the Olympics in 2004, 2008 and 2012, as well as in four consecutive World Championships between 2003 and 2011, she has shown the rare aptitude to exhibit both great team-work, as well as individual flair.

Her journey started at St. Thomas Aquinas High School in Fort Lauderdale, Florida, where her outstanding academic successes (4.0 grade point average) dove-tailed with her track and field commitments, which led her being crowned National High School Female Athlete of the Year, USA Track and Field's Youth Athlete of the Year, and Track and Field News Women's Prep Athlete of the Year in 2002.

That special year was also when she became a naturalised American citizen.

A clever businesswoman, Richards-Ross, along with Jeremy Wariner and Asafa Powell, earned a total of $250,000 in 2006 from the IAAF Golden League by winning all six 400m events throughout that season.

Additionally, on the back of an epic double gold medal haul, in the 400m and 4x400m in the 2009 Berlin World Championships, Richards-Ross set new leading times in Golden League meetings in Zurich and Brussels, to win a share of the $1million cash jackpot for the third time.

Part of Richards-Ross' legacy is that she has shown aspiring female sprinters that you can be highly educated, alluring and also win medals through pain-staking preparation; her continued success are in stark contrast to her humble beginnings.

A born winner if ever there was one, Richards-Ross is a credit to the island from which she came.

Did you know?
- Richards-Ross graduated from the University of Texas at Austin in 2006 with a degree in management information systems
- In February 2010, Richards-Ross married American Football player Aaron Ross, and it was featured on an episode of TV show, Platinum Weddings.

Lawrence Rowe

Born: January 8, 1949

Place of birth: Kingston

As Test debuts go, Lawrence Rowe's was perfection personified. He made his international bow against New Zealand in February 1972 and notched 214 and 100 not out at Sabina Park in his two innings.

It was the first time that a cricketer had scored a double and single century on Test debut. It also gave him a batting average of 314 after his first Test match.

Rowe did not go on to totally fufil his early promise having made his debut for Jamaica in 1968–69 but the blistering start to his Test career has ensured his place in the record books forever.

He was an enigmatic, elegant, composed right-hander, opening or high in the order. He had a penchant for scoring heavily at his home ground, Sabina Park. In 1974 against England he scored 302 in a marathon knock of 10 hours. Only three other West Indian batsmen have scored a triple century, the others being Garfield Sobers, Chris Gayle and Brian Lara.

Having announced himself to the cricket world, Rowe toured Australia in 1975–76 as arguably the best batsman in the world. A century in his second Test innings in Australia maintained his average at over 70 runs per innings and it seemed to confirm his reputation.

However, Clive Lloyd's men were annihilated by Dennis Lillee and Jeff Thompson and Rowe's confidence was shattered. He was never the same again.

Former teammate Michael Holding, who knew a thing or two about world class batsmen during a career spent trying to dismantle them, was once of the opinion that Rowe was "the best batsman I ever saw", and that "I could not imagine anyone ever batting better or being able to".

The Jamaican batsman was to court controversy towards the end of his career. Rowe, when past his prime, became infamous in 1982–83, because

he led a rebel tour to South Africa during the days of apartheid when they were isolated from world sport.

The West Indian public were outraged by the tour and Rowe himself and others were ostracised in Jamaica. This may have been a primary reason for Rowe subsequently settling in Miami, USA

Did You Know...?
- Rowe's career was hindered by an allergy to grass
- Rowe once initiated legal action against the Jamaica Cricket Association (JCA) for revoking its decision to name the pavilion at Sabina Park in Kingston after him
- In 2004, Rowe was named among Jamaica's five greatest cricketers of all time. The others were George Headley, Michael Holding, Courtney Walsh and Jeff Dujon

Tessa Sanderson

Born: March 14, 1956

Place of birth: St. Elizabeth

Tessa Sanderson, one of Great Britain's greatest ever Olympians, was actually born in Jamaica. Sanderson competed in the javelin competition in every one of the six Olympics from 1976-1996. Only one other athlete, in the long and glorious history of the Games, has managed such a feat, discus thrower Lia Manoliu from the Republic of Moldova.

Sanderson, who also has Ghanaian heritage, was to land a coveted Olympic gold medal at the 1984 Olympic Games in Los Angeles, becoming the first British black woman ever to do so.

Sanderson, who after retirement has been keen to help young people understand the positive nature of sport by setting up her own Foundation and academy, had given plenty of indicators as to her burgeoning potential prior to landing gold in the United States.

In 1974 she claimed gold at the Commonwealth Games in Edmonton, Canada. And just to prove that she was not prepared to rest on her laurels after Los Angeles, she went on to win two more Commonwealth titles in 1986 and 1990.

There was generally always a smile on Sanderson's face but it did not disguise that she was a fierce competitor.

Sanderson, who represented the Wolverhampton & Bilston and Borough of Hounslow athletics clubs, had an intense rivalry with fellow Briton Fatima Whitbread. Although Whitbread was superior between 1984 and 1987, overall Sanderson had a 27-18 advantage in their head-to-head clashes between 1977 and 1988. It was sport at its very best as the two did battle over the years.

Their personal battles were never more stark than at the Meadowbank Stadium in Glasgow, Scotland in 1986 when Sanderson pipped Whitbread to gold in an astonishing competition at the Commonwealth Games.

Sanderson won it in the penultimate round with 69.80m to overtake Whitbread's 68.54m; as the winner celebrated, the silver-medallist sat on the ground in despair. It was sport showing its greatest emotion.

Sanderson decided to retire from athletics at the World Championships in 1997. Numerous TV appearances have ensued.

In 1984 she decided to use her experience to help others. The Tessa Sanderson Foundation and Academy, is a charity, and was set up to assist young people in sport, promote a healthier lifestyle and through physical activity, together with building confidence and a social wellbeing whilst still in education.

Did you know?

- Sanderson has been recipient of the MBE, OBE and CBE in the Queen's honours list
- The javelin ace remains the only British woman to ever win a throwing gold medal
- On May 1, 2010, Sanderson married Densign White who is currently chairman of British Judo and Strategic Director of the European Judo Federation who competed in three Olympic Games and is also a Commonwealth Games gold medallist

Trecia Keye-Smith

Born: November 5, 1975

Place of Birth: Westmoreland, St Elizabeth

Superlatives are simply not enough to describe the outstanding contribution the selfless and ultra-committed triple-jumper has made to athletics, nationally and internationally.

The youngest of four, her triumph of being the first Caribbean female triple jumper to win a global title has left a precious legacy inspiring participation increases in the event from kids from the region.

The 15-time All-American title holder, was brought up playing netball and competing in track & field but it was in the latter where she made her name, representing the University of Pittsburgh as a seven-time NCAA national champion in outdoor and indoor long and triple jump competitions respectively.

Seemingly self-effacing, Smith, no stranger to hard work during her humble formative years, begun racing competitively aged 15 years of age, but the experience clearly put her in good stead as she was named 'Most Outstanding Student-Athlete' by the NCAA National Championships while at college.

Peaking in 2005 when becoming world champion in Helsinki, she then routinely added back-to-back Commonwealth gold medals to her collection in Melbourne 2006 and Delhi 2010.

After her stunning achievements in India, Smith was awarded with the David Dixon Award at the closing ceremony of the 19th Commonwealth Games, providing the cherry on her proverbial cake of championship success.

With a personal best of 15.16m, the coveted award rewarded her tireless endeavour and superb record of medalling in all her three performances at Commonwealth Games, including a bronze medal in Manchester 2002.

Her love of sport has found her working on the other side of the track as well, as a physiotherapist. Therefore, after a hard day of competing herself, she'd retreat to helping the best coaches prepare the nation's future athletes.

Despite living in London, for a significant chunk of her life, Smith's rejected any notion of representing Great Britain, continuing to echo her pride of competing for the country of her birth and upbringing.

Did you know?
- As well as successfully completing a Master's degree in Physiotherapy, Smith also attained a Bachelor of Science in Exercise Science whilst at the University of Pittsburgh, Pennsylvania.
- Smith was once member of British track outfit, Shaftesbury Barnet Harriers in London.
- Smith has also been involved in coaching, lending her considerable experience to her British training partners.

Bunny Sterling

Born: April 4, 1948
Place of birth: Jamaica

Black British boxers owe a debt of gratitude to Bunny Sterling. The Jamaica-born middleweight became the first immigrant to win a British title when Mark Rowe's wounded eye brought their bout to a fourth round conclusion at Wembley Arena on September 8, 1970.

Sterling, who also claimed the Commonwealth middleweight title that evening, offers more than a statistical curiosity as his success ultimately enabled future black boxing contenders to win British belts that were seen as the preserve of white fighters.

In 1956 Sterling came to England, aged 12, with his sister following the death of their grandmother.

He displayed an aptitude for rugby and athletics but by the time Sterling was 15 he was fighting as an amateur and was still only 17-years-old on his professional debut in 1966.

The youngster lost his first three fights on points but the turnaround came in December that year, when he avenged his defeat to Fess Parker just two months after their first meeting.

Sterling won his next 13 consecutive bouts and won the Southern Area middleweight title at his second attempt with an eighth round TKO of Johnny Kramer on November 11, 1968.

Kramer had defeated Sterling six months earlier but had no answer this time to the Jamaican's superior footwork.

It would be almost two years before he got the title shot he craved. The man himself is in no doubt regarding the motives of the authorities.

"It was assumed that I would be beaten, which would prevent me, if I was beaten, to fight for the full title, and also to stop me becoming a part of the English history," he told the Caribbean Boys in Care website.

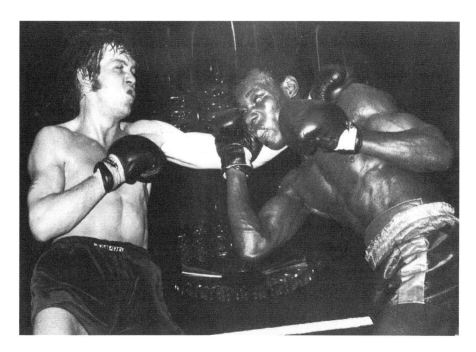

Sterling earned a Lonsdale belt on the way to defending his title on five occasions.

He also contested the European middleweight title three times. His first shot came in 1971 when he suffered a 14th round knockout to Jean-Claude Bouttier in Paris. In the second, Elio Calcabrini won a points decision when the pair met in Milan in 1973.

The European success that eluded him came on February 20, 1976 when he met Germany's Frankie Reiche in Hamburg for the now vacant title. Sterling forced a 13th round stoppage that cemented his legacy.

He finished with a record of 35 wins (14 KO), 18 defeats and four draws.

Did You Know?
- Sterling never had a promoter
- His only fight in his homeland came in 1972 when he drew with Roy Lee at the National Arena in Kingston
- Sterling was the only black child at his boarding school in London

Stafanie Taylor

Born: June 11, 1991
Place of birth: Spanish Town

It would be fair to say that the prodigiously talented Stefanie Taylor would do herself justice in the men's West Indies cricket team.

Taylor is the female version of West Indies' one-day captain Dwayne Bravo; she makes runs, takes wickets and is excellent in the field and is still in her infancy at the age of 22.

Taylor made her debut for West Indies at 17, against Ireland on their tour of Europe on June 24, 2008. She clearly has a sense of occasion, notching 90 runs from just 49 deliveries on her Twenty20 debut. She has not looked back since.

The right-handed batsman and off break bowler, is without question the best female cricketer to be produced by the Caribbean region.

The exciting Taylor's career has many highlights. After her notable debut innings against the Irish she then scored her first half-century in one-day international cricket in her next match against the same opposition.

On this occasion she scored 66 runs from 97 balls. She scored another half-century in her next appearance, scoring 70 runs against the Netherlands.

During the 2009 Women's Cricket World Cup, she was the West Indies best performer, leading the team in both runs scored and wickets taken. She repeated the feat at the 2009 ICC Women's World Twenty20, in which she scored half-centuries in her side's opening two matches to become the only woman to score fifties in three consecutive Twenty20 Internationals, a feat she repeated in 2010 in a three match series against Sri Lanka.

She scored her maiden century in one-day internationals in October 2009, hitting 108 not out against South Africa.

Her fine form saw her average, at the start of September 2013, 45.88 in one-day internationals and 33.53 in the T20 version of the game

It was no surprise then that accolades would follow for Taylor. She was named ICC Women's ODI Cricketer of the Year in 2012 having won the Women's Cricketer of the Year award in 2011.

Despite having a glorious career still ahead of her, Taylor is already "giving back" and is keen to promote the sport to other women in the region.

She is actively encouraging young girls to take up the sport. While the boys want to emulate the likes of Chris Gayle, the girls have their own heroine in Taylor.

Did You Know?

- Stafanie was just 10 when she went on her first cricket tour, from Jamaica to Guyana
- Her middle name is Roxann

Alf Valentine

Born: April 28, 1930 – May 11, 2004
Place of birth: Kingston

Few cricketers can lay claim to songs written in their honour. Alf Valentine, the first West Indies bowler to take 100 Test wickets, and his colleague Sonny Ramadhin were honoured in the chorus of Lord Beginner's Victory Calypso, which commemorated the tourists' first-ever Test victory in England in 1950.

'Second Test and West Indies won, with those two little pals of mine, Ramadhin and Valentine.'

The tall 20-year-old left-arm spinner took seven wickets as the West Indies won by 326 runs.

It followed the 11 wickets taken on his Test debut at Old Trafford. Both he and fellow spinner Ramadhin made their names during that tour, which saw the West Indies clinch a 3-1 victory and Valentine take 33 wickets in four Tests.

The Kingston native had served notice that the West Indies' threat stretched beyond the Three Ws of Frank Worrell, Clyde Walcott and Everton Weekes.

Such was their reliance upon their spin twins during that tour that Valentine bowled 1185.2 overs across the whole tour and Ramadhin himself exceeded 1000. Inevitably both men were named as Wisden Cricketers of the Year.

Remarkably, both men had only completed two first class matches prior to their selection – the trial matches for the tour – and Valentine had nabbed only two wickets for 190 runs.

Yet some prescient soul saw fit to rubber stamp his call-up and soon he was demonstrating his ability to turn the ball beguilingly from round the wicket at considerable pace.

It was also during this tour that the short-sighted Jamaican obtained the glasses that became synonymous with his image.

That summer was to prove the zenith of his international career, although he still took 24 Test wickets in Australia in 1951-52 and went on to clinch 139 wickets in 36 Tests at a reasonable 30.32 runs and was also involved in the momentous first Tied Test in Brisbane in 1960.

Injuries and illness did much to curtail his involvement, as did the emergence of Lance Gibbs, but perhaps Valentine's finest achievements came away from the field.

During the 1960-61 tour of Australia a chance visit to a children's home made him want to devote his life to helping underprivileged kids.

The widower Valentine moved to the United States with second wife and the couple became foster parents to a succession of abandoned children.

In 2004 Valentine suffered a stroke and died shortly after, aged 74. His legacy within the West Indies' first great team had been long assured.

Did you know?

- Valentine's 33 wickets in four Tests during the 1950 tour of England remained a West Indies record until it was beaten by Malcolm Marshall in 1988
- The 92 overs he sent down in the second innings at Trent Brige during the third Test in 1950 remained a record until eclipsed by Ramadhin's 97 overs at Edgbaston in 1957

Melaine Walker

Born: January 1, 1983

Place of Birth: Rosetown, Kingston

To adopt a striking hairstyle whilst competing in front of millions of people at the highest level of sport means that you have to be good at your discipline. And 400m hurdler Melaine Walker certainly was.

Donning an eye-catching short cut spikey-topped pineapple-esque mane, Walker most notably stole the show by floating through the pack to take the Olympic gold medal in Beijing's Birds Nest stadium in 2008 – setting a new Games record in the process of 52.64 seconds.

Eager to show her dominance over the discipline, the former St Jago High runner became national champion the following year finishing the race 6/100th of second short of her sensational Beijing time, while qualifying for her first World Championship in the process.

For a consecutive major championships Walker's infectious smile stole the hearts of the thousands of people that filled the Berlin stadium at the World Championships, but it wasn't her smile that left them awestruck. Walker blew the competition away to record a stunning time of 52.42s – the second fastest time in history.

Even the championship mascot, aptly named, Berlino the Bear was 'over-roared' by the scintillating display by Walker, inadvertently crashing into a cart of hurdles whilst 'piggy backing' the victor on her victory lap. Ouch!

Still with the world at her feet, she admitted, during an interview with The Gleaner, that she "never thought it would happen so early". Indeed, Walker was a great junior but her achievements have extended further into her senior career than many anticipated.

For Walker, it may be a case of fate, as she was forced to move from flat sprinting to hurdles in order to adapt to previous major injuries.

She had won bronze and silver medals at the World Junior Champion-ships, and moved to the United States to attend Essex County College and the University of Texas.

Keeping up the tradition of winning Jamaican participants in the hur-dles, Walker is at the precipice of greatness and frighteningly for her oppo-nents observers predict that most of her best days are yet to come.

Did you know?

- For her achievements in Beijing 2008, Walker was named, alongside world record holder Usain Bolt, Athlete of the Year.
- In Beijing, she was dominant. Her run of 52.42 seconds broke the national record set by Deon Hemmings in Atlanta and established a new Olympic record.
- As part of an anti-violence community campaign, Walker has hosted a series of parties in Rose Town under her name to raise money to help restore a youth club in the area, just one of the positive initiatives she's involved in.

Courtney Walsh

Born: October 30, 1962

Place of Birth: Kingston

West Indies cricket has been blessed with a plethora of world class fast bowlers. It could be argued that Courtney Walsh was the very best. Career highlights for Walsh were plentiful. One of his proudest took place in 2000 when Walsh created history by becoming the first bowler to take 500 Test wickets. Many bowlers have since passed 500 wickets in the ultimate format of the game but the affable Walsh has the distinction of reaching the landmark before anyone else in a sport where statistics are king.

Bowling in the second Test between West Indies and South Africa in Port-of-Spain, Trinidad, Walsh took the wicket of Gary Kirsten, caught behind, to move to 499 victims before trapping the much respected Jacques Kallis lbw just two balls later to reach the magical 500 figure.

Walsh had made his Test debut against Australia at Perth in 1984 and went on to claim 519 wickets in total.

The lanky Jamaica had got into the West Indies team after the stellar careers of Michael Holding, Malcolm Marshall and Joel Garner. He was to prove to be a skilled workhorse bowling 30,019 deliveries in a 17-year Test career.

Walsh is one of only four bowlers to have bowled over 5,000 overs in Test cricket, the others significantly being three spinners; Muttiah Muralitharan of Sri Lanka and Shane Warne of Australia, and Anil Kumble of India.

His partnership and great wicket-taking success with fellow quick, Curtly Ambrose, saw the pair take 421 wickets in 49 Tests. In one-day cricket, Walsh made 205 appearances taking 227 wickets.

Unusually for a fast bowler, Walsh was named West Indies captain in 1994 to confirm the high regard in which he was held. When not perform-

ing for West Indies, Walsh was serving English county Gloucestershire between 1984-1998.

Fellow fast bowler Colin Croft once said of Walsh, and summed up the views of most in the Caribbean: "There will never be another Courtney Walsh." In 1993 Walsh was awarded the Order of Jamaica (OJ), Jamaica's third highest national honour.

Walsh probably bowled faster for longer than any man in history. Like a fine wine he simply got better with age.

Did you know?

- During his Test career, Walsh had a miserly economy rate of just 2.54
- Walsh's poor batting earned him a record 43 ducks in Test cricket
- The Jamaican was named Wisden Cricketer of the Year in 1987

Warren Weir

Born: October 31, 1989

Place of Birth: Trelawny, Jamaica

For many track and field fans, it was a case of: 'Warren who?' as the former hurdler catapulted his way into the public consciousness with a series of outstanding sprint performances during 2012.

With the world's spotlight firmly shone upon his record-breaking compatriots Usain Bolt and Yohan Blake as the trio stood in the blocks of the 200m sprint final at the London 2012 Olympic Games, little was known, let alone expected from the Trelawny native.

However, as his two fellow Jamaicans stretched the field to take the victory and runner-up position, the 22 year-old fought and harried across the track to secure a priceless bronze medal – with the result that Jamaica landed a clean sweep of medals in the 200m, a mind-blowing achievement for a nation of just 2.7million, on the world's biggest sporting stage.

Personally, the achievement meant even more for Weir. Alongside, the joys of standing on the podium and partaking in a lap of honour in front of a packed 80,000 London Olympic Stadium beside living legends, it was easy to forget that this was only Weir's first major international senior tournament, a truly staggering achievement.

Fending off the best of what the Americans and Europeans had to offer, in the form of Wallace Spearman and Christophe Lemaitre respectively, he propelled himself into world class status, leaving many shocked faces in his wake.

The baby-faced Racers Track Club athlete recorded a personal best time of 19.84 seconds, despite only breaking 21 seconds for the first time in the Jamaican Championships in 2011, heralding a remarkable upturn in performance.

Weir's interest in athletics begun in the 110m hurdles, and he also participated in the shorter sprint distances of 100m and 200m representing Calabar High School at the Jamaican High School Championships.

A finalist in the hurdles at the 2007 Pan American Junior Athletics Championships, Weir's rise was prompted by his second-place finish at the 2008 CARIFTA Games in addition to 4x100m relay gold success.

Boosted by a respectable junior athletics education, Weir transformed into a 200m sprint specialist in 2011 under the wing of famed Jamaican coach Glen Mills, after it was believed the hurdles was negatively affecting him in terms of knee injuries.

Like a duck to water, Weir performed well in his first Diamond League meeting in London, he recorded a personal best of 20.43 seconds, finishing second behind Beijing 2008 Olympic Games 100m and 200m bronze medallist Walter Dix - before again improving his personal best down to 20.08s in June 2012.

Putting to bed any doubts about whether or not he had the staying power to consistently perform at the sharp end of the sport, Weir's 200m silver and 4x100m relay gold at the 2013 World Championships in Moscow, cemented his status as yet another Jamaican sprinting protégé to turn promise into medals.

Did you know?

- Football mad Weir is a Chelsea supporter. He was also invited down to west London club following his memorable run at the London Olympics.
- He is known for saying "No English, straight Patois," sparking calls on social networks for T-shirts to be printed with the phrase.

Theodore Whitmore

Born: August 5 1972

Place of birth: Montego Bay

Every team needs a Theodore Whitmore type player and it's universally recognised that had the midfielder affectionately known as 'Tappa' not been in the famous 1998 Reggae Boyz squad, they may not have even made it to France for the World Cup.

Whitmore was named as part of the first ever English speaking Caribbean side to reach the finals of the World Cup in 1998 and cemented his legacy by scoring two goals against Japan.

The former Violet Kickers and Seba United player has always had the Midas touch but he was appreciated as a player as much for his skill and guile as he was for his battling and leadership qualities.

Unsurprisingly his game attracted the attention of English clubs where he went onto ply his trade at Hull City and Tranmere Rovers. Whitmore did a brief stint in Scotland with Livingston but his love affair with Jamaica was to be rekindled when he returned to his roots at Seba United in 2006 as manager.

Having had two brief periods as interim head coach of the national team Whitmore's march into management was vindicated when he was handed a three-year contract in 2011 having helped Jamaica to land the 2010 Digicel Cup title.

The decision to retain Whitmore as head coach was taken during a revamping of the overall Jamaican Football Federation's structure and with a view to preserving some continuity ahead of the 2014 World Cup in Brazil.

However, in June 2013 Whitmore's love affair with Jamaican football came to a temporary halt when his untenable position as head coach of Jamaica ended with his resignation after 58 games at the helm.

The 40-year-old was pushed into a corner by the Jamaican Football Federation (JFF) to either resign or be sacked following the third World Cup qualifying defeat over a dismal eight day spell for the Reggae Boyz.

But it was his side's lacklustre display in their torrid 2-0 defeat at the Honduras National Stadium that was the final nail in the coffin.

Previously there were calls for Whitmore to leave his J$1M (£6,400) a month role following a string of poor results that put their dreams of qualifying for the World Cup in Brazil in severe jeopardy.

Whitmore was rushed into an emergency meeting with JFF president Captain Horace Burrell just two hours after the final whistle in Tegucigalpa, and Whitmore claimed that he was asked to resign and had every intention to do so.

Did you know?

- In 1998 Theodore Whitmore was named Caribbean Footballer of the Year.
- As a player Whitmore gained 105 caps and scored 24 goals for his country.

Arthur Wint

Born: May 25, 1920 – October 19, 1992

Place of birth: Plowden, Manchester, Jamaica

Multi-talented, multi-faceted and a gentle giant, the world today could learn a thing or two from Arthur Wint, Jamaica's first ever Olympic gold medalist.

Wint's motto 'you makes your choices', quite literally summed the big man up.

Standing at 6' 6", Wint's imposing figure meant he impacted on people's lives even when he wasn't trying to.

His formative years saw him attend Calabar High School for Boys, an institution with a rich history in track and field and the beginning of his athletics career.

However, sport wasn't the only thing on Wint's mind. His mother and father, a school teacher and minister respectively, instilled a work ethic in Wint which would go on to hold the future star in good stead.

The second of five children, two girls and three boys, Wint, along with two of his brothers joined the Royal Air Force aged 22 despite showing promise in a range of athletics events.

He still maintained an interest in sport and by the time he had become a fully trained pilot in 1944 he'd also managed to etch his name into history by running the fastest 400m time in Canada, were he was doing his pilot training.

Managing a sporting interest and pursuing a vocation wasn't easy and Wint's ultimate test came when he was sent to England for the Second World War.

By the end of the war however, Wint had not only been promoted to Flight Lieutenant he'd also left the RAF and moved to St Barts Hospital in London as a medical student on a scholarship.

His finest sporting hour came at the London 1948 Olympic Games where Wint stormed to a gold in the 400m and he wasn't done there.

Wint went on to win gold again as part of Jamaica's 4x400m relay team at the Helsinki Olympic Games in 1952 as well as a silver medal in the 800m.

A truly remarkable character, Jamaicans the world over recognise Wint as one of the founding fathers of their present day successes.

Did you know?

- On his way to winning Jamaica's first ever Olympic gold Wint set a new world record in the 400m in a time of 46. 2 seconds.
- While on active service in England, Wint represented the RAF, the Polytechnics Harriers Athletics Club and the Combined Services and Great Britain.
- A street in Kingston is named Arthur Wint Drive in his honour.